Moments
from the
Mountainside

Jack A Droste
Joshua 24:15
Matthew 25:35-40

Jack Droste

ISBN 978-1-0980-7188-2 (paperback)
ISBN 978-1-0980-7189-9 (digital)

Christian Faith Publishing, Inc.
832 Park Avenue
Meadville, PA 16335
www.christianfaithpublishing.com

Printed in the United States of America

Contents

Acknowledgment 5

Introduction...7

The Road Less Traveled—Matthew 7:13–14 10
Heaven on Earth—1 Corinthians 2:9...15
Driving through the Fog—Job 1:8 18
The Potter's Wheel—Jeremiah 18:2–6...22
Before Time Began—1 Peter 1:18–20 26
A Very Present Help—Psalm 46:1–7 30
From the East to the West—Ephesians 3:18, Psalm 103:12.........34
Tears of a Broken Heart—Daniel 3:22, 25 39
The Glories of His Majesty—John 21:25 43
Change of Plans—1 Samuel 14:6 45
In the Eye of the Beholder—Ecclesiastes 3:11, 14 48
Bumps and Bruises—Philippians 3:12–14....................................53
God's Timing—Jeremiah 29:11 57
Perspectives—John 4:35 60
Holding on Tightly—Mark 10:17–22..64
Jesus with Skin On—1 Corinthians 9:19–22 68
Faithfully Stay—Matthew 26:37–41 72
Choices—Deuteronomy 30:19–20..74
Perseverance—Judges 6:12, 15; 7:2 78
Treasures—Matthew 6:19–21 82
The Whole World in His Hands—Luke 4:5–8....................................85
Layers—2 Corinthians 11:22–30 89
Like a Bridge—1 Timothy 2:5–6..94
The Lord Is My Shepherd—Psalm 23:1–4 99
White as Snow—Isaiah 1:18 102

The Light of the World—Matthew 5:14–16 105
More than Conquerors—Romans 8:28–39 107
Contrasts—Luke 16:22–24 111
A Living Memorial—Joshua 4:5–7 116
Who We Are—Colossians 3:17 121
A Better Way—Proverbs 3:5–6 125
But Why God Why—Isaiah 9:6 129
Heritage—Joshua 1:5 133
A Way through It—1 Corinthians 10:13 138
You All Are Invited—Revelation 19:7–9 142

Acknowledgment

Throughout the countless hours of writing and rewriting this book, I have always been keenly aware that, though I was the individual who was sitting at the keyboard trying to write the words that I believe my Lord and Savior had laid on my heart, there were two other people to whom this endeavor would not have possible without their support.

To my loving bride of over forty years, Nancy, thank you for believing in me, encouraging me, supporting me, putting up with my incessant babbling about how "I see another one of my stories a coming!" You are the love of my life, and this would have never been possible without you. "A wife of noble character who can find? She is worth far more than rubies" (Prov. 31:10 NIV). Nancy, you are everything that is embodied in the words, "A wife of noble character."

As well, the second person I need to, and want to, express my appreciation to is my mother, Martha E. Brooks. Mom, you aren't here to see this day, but without the way you supported us growing up and taught us that we can do whatever we set our eyes on, this book would have never been possible. Even though the thought of seeing your name in a book probably never crossed your mind, here it is today. Thank you for being the backbone, and "cattle prod" in our family, always encouraging us and prodding us to do our best and to never fear to try something new.

Introduction

As I read my Bible (in particular the four Gospels of the New Testament where we read so much about the life of Jesus Christ), I am impressed with how often the actual words (or expressed thoughts), "The kingdom of heaven is like..." are spoken by Jesus as He lived and walked with the men and women of His day while here on earth. Part of loving each other means we need to communicate with each other. Part of communicating with each other means loving each other enough that we want to communicate in such a way that people can understand, or even develop a mental picture of what it is that we are trying to say. This is the very essence of what a parable is: telling a story in a manner whereby it paints a word picture in the mind of the one hearing our story, which then helps enable them to better understand the truth of what we are hoping to share with them. It is from this desired mindset of wanting to be more like my Lord that I believe this work has sprung forth.

The basic format for *Moments from the Mountainside* began to develop many years ago as I found myself writing stories, or letters, or even rewriting the words to a song so that it might become something very special to the one to whom it was sent. One story was entirely in fun as I described a scene that I had just witnessed of two elk slipping and sliding on an icy roadway. Another story developed from the need to say more in a Valentine's Day card than the words that I could find on a store shelf. Another story was one I wrote in a letter to my mother over forty years ago regarding a speeding ticket I never received and handcuffs that were never used and a time in jail that never happened just so the bad news of a parking ticket that I did receive would be seen in a better perspective and not be seen as being all that bad. Another story told about an older couple who braved the bitter wind and cold of the South Dakota plains as they walked to the local US Post Office in hopes of a long-awaited package, only to realize upon arriving they had both forgotten to bring the mailbox key with them. In each instance, the goal that I had was to try to paint a mental picture for the reader so they would feel as if they were right there in the midst of the scene.

In writing *Moments from the Mountainside*, this author's goal was to try to place the reader in the seat right beside the author as he drove up and down the highways of this beautiful nation we live in so that the reader might be able to envision exactly what the author was seeing. The goal was for the reader to be able to feel the absolute darkness of the ebony-black sky, or the totally blinding effect of the fog, or the warmth of the beautiful rays of the sun, or the vastness of the open prairies along with the author as we drove along so that we could then also better understand the truths of God's Word, which is often seen and experienced in this world that *He* created for us and that we call home.

Come along with me as together we explore the truths that God has for us as we travel up and down the highways and back roads of our land that we call home. What is it that God might be saying to your heart as you see the beauty and magnificence of His handiwork and creation? These are my *Moments from the Mountainside.*

The Road Less Traveled

There are times when my car has just refused to learn the lesson (or if it already knows the lesson, to abide by it) that it is best to follow the path the GPS, or the atlas, or the trip tic tells you is the best route to take. This day would be no different.

We were heading out from the town of Cedaredge, Colorado, on a beautiful late summer day. The temperatures were hovering around the eighty-degree mark. The winds were light, and the skies were clear, with nary a cloud to be seen. Even though this weather would hold true for our twelve-hour 325-mile journey this day, there would be little else that would remain consistent throughout this day.

When we left Cedaredge that morning, we traveled over the Grand Mesa, which lies just to the north of this little town. The Grand Mesa, because of the enormity of its size, is home to over two hundred lakes. The pine and fir trees are plentiful and full. The aspens stood tall and thick in their stands, with all the colors of fall painting the leaves on their branches. The meadows were already decked out in their plush autumn shag carpets of the brightest of greens, yellows, and oranges.

In descending the four thousand feet from the top of the mesa to the desert floors below, the altitude was not the only thing to change. The tall tan tips of the desert grasses waved gently in the breezes below. On top of the mesa, there had been trees in plenty. On the desert floor below, there were few to be seen, where here the desert scrub brush reigned supreme as it dotted the landscape for as far as the eye could see.

As we headed west toward our destination for the day, we settled into our spot in the busy traffic pattern of the interstate. The flow of traffic ran well, and even though it wasn't like a heavy big-city rush hour traffic, it was plentiful. Mile after mile we drove along, being passed by those in pursuit of their agenda for the day and passing those for whom the steepness of the hills was too great. Even though the map told us the exit we needed to take was Exit 182, when we got to Exit 214, we decided this was the turn for us. Both routes would end up taking us to the same destination. It was there, though, the similarities ended.

Almost as soon as we left the interstate, we knew we were in for a different kind of drive that day. Within a hundred yards of the exit, there was a sign warning us of the fact that this road no longer would receive adequate care and maintenance. A few miles further down the road, as we approached the first town we would come to, we found nothing but run-down, dilapidated buildings, weather worn and crumbling, where a small yet thriving community used to meet the needs of the railroad that ran by on the other side of the highway. Whereas the interstate was smooth and wide, this road was narrow and was home to more than one cattle guard we would have to rumble across. Was this the way we wanted to come? Was I sure we had made the right choice in taking this exit? The answer would soon become a resounding yes. Had we not decided to take the road that so many others ignored that day, we would never have been able to enjoy the blessing of driving down through the valley where the mighty Colorado River winds and cuts its way through some of the most beautiful scenery we have ever seen.

As Highway 128 coursed its way down this narrow valley, we found ourselves to be in the constant presence of this mighty river. Though the river was caramel brown in color (from all the silt and dirt it was moving downstream), the bluffs and monoliths that rose hundreds of feet in the air on either side of it were the deepest red sandstone one could imagine. Near the edge of the riverbanks, the juniper trees thrived and had branches filled with their deep-green needles. The boulders that had fallen from the bluffs above were the size of cabins that we had camped in before. The narrow stretch of sky above was the clearest high desert blue one can imagine. If it wasn't for the many times when the only word being uttered was

Wow, we may have driven in nearly complete silence that day. On that day, we were truly blessed with being able to see, and experience the beauty of God's creation in a way that so many others would never know. And it was all because we turned where others didn't, didn't follow where others did, and were willing to take the road less traveled. I believe this is a truth that will hold true in our spiritual lives as well.

In Matthew 7:13–14, Matthew wrote:

> Enter through the narrow gate. For wide is the gate and broad is the road that leads to destruction, and many enter through it. But small is the gate and narrow the road that leads to life, and only a few find it. (NIV)

Here, the apostle is reaffirming to us the message that Luke wrote in Acts when he said, "Salvation is found in no one else, for there is no other name under heaven given to men by which we must be saved" (Acts 4:12 NIV). Whether it is for those of us who have come to a saving relationship with Jesus Christ (through His sacrificial death and resurrection on Calvary's cross) and are in that portion of our journey now or whether it is for those who have yet to come to that part of their journey in life, there is one thing constant for all: we are saved through the merciful grace of a loving Father whose Son died on the cross to pay the price for our sins. When we ask, as the jailer did in Acts 16, "What must I do to be saved?" (Acts 16:30 NIV), we have to be aware that the answer will always be the same: "Believe in the Lord Jesus, and you will be saved" (Acts 16:31 NIV).

I do believe though, that even if we are Christians who are firmly founded in our faith, the verses above from Matthew 7:13–14 hold additional significance for us in our walk and devotion to the One whom we call Lord. Are we as children of the living God willing to say, "Lord, here I am. I am willing to go where *you* need me to go, even if it is to the road less traveled." There are those for whom God's call on their lives will lead them to the masses of people that we all work with and walk with daily. For them, they are following God's call and are right and proper to do so. But what if God is leading you to do that which might not be seen as being "the norm" or which might not be seen as being the place that is normally gone to? Are we willing to turn off the beaten path to see what it is that God has made special for us? Sometimes, that might mean a different destination. Sometimes, it might mean doing a different thing right where you are at. Sometimes, God's road less traveled might even mean reaching out to a hurting person or segment of society in a different way than what others have.

Are we willing to go, and do, where few others have been willing to and see that which God has created especially for us? I pray the answer for all of us is *yes*!

JACK DROSTE

Heaven on Earth

As it is with most people, this day had been way too long in coming. For most of us, the idea of taking the time to take a family vacation is not something that comes high upon the priority list. We have households where, if they are a two-parent household of a single family unit, both parents normally have to work just to make their paychecks stretch from one payday to the next. If we have a two-parent household with a blended family, you have the additional dynamics of visitation and oftentimes additional children to care for and custody issues where getting away is even more difficult. As well, there are those households where there is only a single parent working hard to do the job of two, while oftentimes working multiple jobs, while trying to be mom and dad and coach and chauffer and counselor, among many other jobs. For a pastor, things are no different.

For this pastor and spouse, our day had finally come to take our long-needed vacation. For us, there would be no other place that would capture our interest and love more than going up to the mountains near where we used to live. So we planned and packed and left the cornfields of Iowa behind us as we set our sights on a campground high up in the mountains above Colorado Springs, Colorado. After just a little more than forty-eight hours, and after zigzagging across six states, we arrived at the little cabin that would be our home for the next few days.

The view that we beheld as we sat on the front porch of the cabin could never be adequately described in mere words, in spite of us sitting there in front of it. Reaching out before us, with the base of the two hills rising to each side of it, was a beautiful little valley that would lead us down to the lakes a quarter mile away. In this valley, the lush green grass provided food and protection to the white tail and the mule deer that came down daily to eat their fill. Also, at times, a herd of elk could be seen, working its way through this valley as they looked for a place to rest for the night. Rising up the gentle slope of the hills on each side of this valley were stands of pine trees and aspens. The pine trees stood tall and erect as they reached forty to fifty feet in the air. Their numerous branches were fully loaded with the dark-green needles and cocoa-brown colored pine cones for which they are known. The aspens wore their typical white-barked trunks with pride and demonstrated to all that fall would soon be coming as their leaves were beginning to make the annual change from the bold green of the summer to the lime green and then to the golden-yellow leaves they would wear, before finally shedding them for the winter. Above all this, one had as magnificent of a view of Pike's Peak and the mountain range that it is a part of as one might ever want. At the distance that the range was before us, the fir and pine tree forests looked to be a deep evergreen in color. Occasionally, in the midst of these forests, one might be able to see the outlines of a lush green meadow dotting the landscape. Above the tree line, the barren rocky surface of the mountains was clearly seen, with the beautiful clear-blue Colorado sky filling out the picture from above. As we beheld all that we saw before us, we couldn't help but think that if there was anywhere on earth where God has placed a bit of heaven, we were looking at it from the comfort of our rocking chair on this very deck.

From this perspective, I couldn't help but be reminded of a few verses that the apostle Paul wrote. In 1 Corinthians 2:9, Paul wrote, "However, as it is written: 'No eye has seen, no ear has heard, no mind has conceived what God has prepared for those who love him'" (NIV). Also, the apostle Paul wrote in Romans 1:20 the following words: "For since the creation of the world God's invisible qualities—his eternal power and divine nature—have been clearly seen, being understood from what has been made, so that men are without excuse..." (NIV).

Even as I sat there and looked at the incredible beauty that lay before me, I was reminded that our God is so much greater than anything we can ever imagine. If a picture of God's creation such as this can be so awe inspiring (in spite of the fact that Genesis 3:17 tells us that even the lands of His creation were cursed by the sin of man), what would this visual be like were it not suffering from the blight of man's first sin? If, as Paul tells us in his letter to the Corinthians that we have yet to see and hear and can't even imagine how marvelous the works of our Creator are, what will this same view of this valley look like when our eyes are fully opened to see who our God is and what He can fully do? And yet, according to the letter to the Romans, the picture that lies before us is enough to tell us there is a God and to tell us how marvelous the works of His hands are even though we can't even comprehend the fullness of who He is. What will it be like when we see the fullness of His perfect creation? A creation without blemish or wrinkle. A creation without the blight of sin. A creation which is no longer viewed or marred by the eyesight of sinful man.

In the book of Psalms, King David wrote, "The heavens declare the glory of God; the skies proclaim the work of his hands. Day after day they pour forth speech; night after night they display knowledge" (Ps. 19:1–2 NIV). Isaiah the prophet wrote, "And they were calling to one another 'Holy, holy, holy is the lord Almighty; the whole earth is full of his glory'" (Isa. 6:3 NIV). May we join in with the chorus of the angels of heaven and with others such as King David and the prophet Isaiah and recognize that "the whole earth is full of his glory."

Driving through the Fog

It was a cold January night as we headed out from the little white church that lay about seven miles from the town of Wounded Knee, South Dakota. As a group, we had labored at this church for the last few days, seeking to help the pastor out with some much-needed repairs to her building. However, the time was now done. The days we had available for working had run out, and it was time to take this group of young people back to their homes in sunny, warm Florida, which lay nearly two thousand miles to the southeast of where we now we're at.

After making the very long and very bumpy drive out the two-mile drive through the field from where the church was to where we would meet the road, we turned north as we headed up toward Interstate 90. For the greatest portion of this road, it runs along and through what is known as the southern unit of the Badlands National Park. For the vast majority of the fifty-five-mile drive along this road, the road will either take you on and along the top of the grassy prairie lands where the buttes and hills of the Badlands are always in sight or it will take you down the hill to the valley below where you can see the dried parch land that is much like the barren desert floor but where the Badland spires and peaks rise up into the sky above you.

On this evening, we had just driven up and over the crest of one of these hills in particular. Normally speaking, when you drive this road, with the winter sun low to the horizon behind you, as you break over the upper most portion of this hill, the incredible beauty of the panoramic view that lies before you is a sight that will suck the breath from your lungs as only the most beautiful of sights will do. From this vantage point of the top of the hill, you are able to see the valley of the Badlands stretched out before you for miles before it ascends the wall on the opposing side of the valley floor some five miles away. This evening would offer a variation of this magnificent beauty that has remained a fixture in my memory for all these years.

On this cold, dark January evening, as we drove along this road, we were bathed in the incredible warmth of the light of the nearly full moon above as it reflected off the purity of the freshly fallen snow that covered the grasslands and prairies below. In spite of the light of the moon shining down on the snow below, and without any light pollution from city lights for at least fifty miles in any direction, even the stars above testified of their existence, as if they were a million different blinking Christmas lights crying out, "Here we are." The final pieces of this beautiful painting though only appeared as we drove up to the crest of the hill before us and looked down into the valley below.

The light of the moon still shone down on the peaks and hills below. The blanket of snow that covered the land as a freshly washed sheet was still evident wherever we looked. The stars twinkled and danced in their far-off locations. But there, hanging in the skies between the moon and stars above and the snow-covered ground below, was a thin layer of dense fog separating the two expanses as if it were a giant down-filled comforter stretched from corner to corner. Above the fog bank, it was a clear night sky with the moon and stars shining down from above. Once you drove partway down the hill, you entered the fog bank and could see little around you. A few moments later, as you exited the fog bank, you were treated to the beauty of the snow-covered peaks and mounds of the Badlands but with what looked like an overcast sky above.

As we make our journeys down the road of our Christian experience, we may find there are times in our lives that are very similar to the views we had of the road on this cold, dark night. We may be enjoying the path we are currently on. We are traveling along, accomplishing and enjoying each task as it comes along. We may even be sinking into that groove of being behind the wheel and seeing mile after mile of beautiful landscape passing by our window. But then the fog hits. Sometimes it may last but for a moment. Other times it may last much longer. Regardless of how long, we feel like we are surrounded by this great cloud bank that keeps us from seeing our future destination. The effect is the same: We fear. We question. We look for help in understanding what has happened and where we are at.

The Bible tells us about a man who once lived and experienced a very similar situation. In Job 1:8, we read where God spoke these words to Satan regarding Job, "Have you considered my servant Job? There is no one on earth like him; he is blameless and upright, a man who fears God and shuns evil" (Job 1:8 NIV). Can you imagine what it must have been like when Job found out that God so trusted Job's relationship with Him that He could brag about Job to others? As we continue reading this section, we can read where Job would go on to lose nearly all he had, including all his family, except his wife. Job went from being in the driver's seat to hitting a fog bank like he had never known. In verse 2:3, it says that Job "maintains his integrity" (Job 2:3 NIV). Though Job couldn't see what had happened, or why it had happened, or maybe even where he was at, the Bible tells us, "Job did not sin in what he said" (Job 2:10 NIV).

There are times when we will find ourselves in a situation very similar to that which Job was in. Where once, we were in a well-lit pathway, we now find ourselves in the thickest, densest fog we could imagine. We may not see more than just a few feet in front of us. But just as Job did, we must hang on to that relationship with our Heavenly Father that got us to where we now are at. We may not understand, but we can continue to trust. We must trust, and we must go on. When Jesus healed the paralytic man who had been lowered down through the roof to him, Jesus told him, "Get up, take your mat and go home" (Mark 2:11 NIV). To continue to lie there after Jesus had healed him was not an option. He was told to go.

For us, stopping in the middle of a fog bank, in the middle of the road, in the middle of the night, is never an option. We must go on. The view may not be the same as what we were just enjoying, but we must go on. It may be different, but we must go on. Only by continuing through the fog of the night can we rise to the hillside on the opposite side of the valley and see the stars and the moon above once more. Perhaps then, and only then, will we be able to see and understand through what and from where our God has brought us. We must go on!

The Potter's Wheel

As we pulled out from the motel in the early hours of this morning, we fully understood that the palate of the scenery that we would observe today would be changing with nearly every mile we would drive. Here, in eastern Kansas, the skies were the lightest of blues with the clouds looking like a fluffy, bright, white cotton ball with a gray shadowy underlining. As we left the metropolitan area, where the traffic of the interstate roared overhead, we left the population base behind. Gone would be our traffic jams, the stoplights, and the wall-to-wall people. Soon to be gone were also the neatly planted rows of the richest and healthiest cornfields one could imagine. Whereas one cornfield might still be the deepest of greens, the next field might be in its early stages of firing, and the next field might be only a field of light tan stalks cut nearly to the ground with its precious commodity having already been harvested. On either side of the road, one might also catch sight of one of the thick fully grown fields of soybeans, where many of the fields could be seen as through the lens of a kaleidoscope, with every hue of yellow and gold and of every shade of green one can imagine.

As we continued our trek west, we noticed that we were seeing fewer and fewer corn and soybean fields and the fields of milo grain were beginning to become more numerous. From one horizon to the next, the brick-red tassels of the milo plant carpeted the land. The upper leaves, where the sunlight was still able to break through the coverage of the red tassels above, were a lighter lime green as compared to the deeper-green stalks and leaves where the sunlight wasn't able to penetrate to. Even as the crops began to change, we also noticed a change in how often we might see fields that were undeveloped, looking much more like the upper deserts of further west than the bountiful croplands of the east.

After many miles and hours of driving, we soon left the croplands entirely behind. No longer would we see the bountiful food supplies of corn and soybeans that would give life and nourishment to all who would eat their fruit. Even so, we no longer would see the thousands and thousands of acres that gave life to the fields of milo that would bring life and strength to the livestock that would then become food to so many. Instead, where the greenery of life once stood tall and strong, we now began to see the tans and browns of the desert lands of western Oklahoma and upper New Mexico. Where the lands were once flat enough that nothing hindered your view of the horizon except the crops of the fields, they would gradually change to rolling hills no taller than perhaps six to ten feet in height and then onward to the mountains and bluffs that rose above the scrub brush and grasses below.

When I gave thought to how our journey would change so dramatically, and so often in just this one day's drive, I was reminded of what God said to the prophet Jeremiah in Jeremiah 18:2–6. Here it is written:

> "Go down to the potter's house, and there I will give you my message." So I went down to the potter's house, and I saw him working at the wheel. But the pot he was shaping from the clay was marred in his hands; so the potter formed it into another pot, shaping it as seemed best to him. Then the word of the Lord came to me: "O house of Israel, can I not do with you as this potter does?" declares the LORD. "Like clay in the hand of the potter, so are you in my hand, O house of Israel." (NIV)

Whether it is through a maturity in our physical age or a growth or maturity in our mental, emotional, or spiritual lives, there is one constant in life. It will be forever changing. Sometimes we may find the activities of our life changing and though we may find that to be difficult, ultimately, we usually are able to cope with the concept of change and adjust our expectations so that we are able to still live life comfortably. We may relocate or move from one home to another. Though it may take a while to learn how to navigate through our new surroundings and community, we usually can make that change. Sometimes change may come in the form of a new job or career. There will be different tasks to learn and different people to get to know. There will even be a different culture for our new place of employment. But we will adapt and change. Sometimes change may even come through the hand of nature or tragedies that are forced upon us. These unexpected changes are oftentimes the most difficult to handle, but again, we learn to adapt and to accept and to go on with our lives. Where the difficulty arises is when we personally are what needs to be changed.

In those verses shared above, God was asking Jeremiah, or challenging him, to allow God to change him even as the potter has the freedom to change and re-change the clay with which he works as he best knows how. Perhaps, as is in this case in Jeremiah, the potter felt the clay pot was marred; so he brought it down and started over the process of gently molding it in his hands until it became something he knew would be useful. Are there not ways that each of us can see in which we might label our own lives marred? Are there ways in which we can even say of ourselves, "Were it not for this (or for that), I could…?" God's desire for His children is for them to be whole and complete, vessels or tools that He can use.

However, there are also things in each of our lives that I believe God desires to help us work through in order that we can better be able to serve him or be used by Him so that He can use us to reach others. Here in Jeremiah, God was asking His prophet, "Will you let *Me* fine tune you in order that you might become an instrument or tool for *Me* to draw others back to a relationship with *Me*?"

Whether we are newly coming to a faith in Jesus Christ as Savior and Lord or whether we are established to some level in our walk with Him, God desires to have a people whom *He* can call his own and whom *He* can use to bring others back to a restored relationship with Him. The clay on the potter's wheel became a useful instrument as it was shaped and reshaped by the hands of the master. Are we willing to let the Master do the same to us by the touch of His loving hands?

Before Time Began

Tonight was a night that was going to be different than many of the other nights I would travel back down the mountainside on my way home. I was tired, and the fatigue of the busyness of the last couple of weeks was setting in. I didn't want to think about writing tonight, or about school, or the business of the church, or about anything else. I just planned on making that thirty-seven-mile drive home and getting it done with. I knew what mile marker I started at and what mile marker I would need to end up at. I could tell you how many curves there were between each of the towns I would go through. I could probably even tell you how many hills I would need to go up and down and where they were at.

As I made it through the first of the many curves and turns I would navigate in the first few miles of my journey, a simple prayer passed over my lips. "Lord, I haven't seen any of the big bull elk in a while. Let me see one." Even though this valley is home to a great number of these awesome creatures, there may be times when I would go for days or weeks without seeing any on either my trip to the camp or on my trip home. Sometimes though, I am still foolish enough to believe God still wants to honor the prayers of His children and bless them in little ways we never deserve. This was one of those moments for me.

Imagine my joy, as just a mile or two later, the headlights of my truck illuminated a pair of magnificent bull elk standing on the road in front of me. Slowly, as if in their minds they owned the road and everything that surrounded it, they purposefully finished traversing the road and walked up to the fence line that separated the roadway from the fields beyond. Effortlessly, and in a single fluid motion, these majestic creatures lifted up their front legs and propelled them-selves over the fence. Upon landing, which was accomplished as silently as was the lift off, they continued their journey off into the darkness of the night and the fields beyond. As I watched this sight unfold in front of me, "Thank You, Lord," were the only words I could think to say.

Here, in the darkness of this night, God answered the prayer of a tired and weary old man. It was a prayer that wasn't earth-shatter-ing. It was a prayer that would have no impact on whether someone would live or die. There was no reason why God had to do what He did by letting me see this sight this night. But He did. And all I could do was humbly say, "Thank You!"

As I thought about this blessing and joy, while continuing my drive down the highway, there was an even greater truth that came to mind. If indeed, those few seconds of being able to see that mighty beast at that specific moment in time was a direct answer to prayer, there was much more to this blessing than just what those few seconds involved. Sometimes when we look at the movement of the hand of God, we fixate our gaze at only the final and finishing act of His handiwork. Most often we fail to realize what must have happened in the past to lead up to the moment that we have just witnessed.

When we see the beauty of the rose, we marvel at how it is a testimony of His workmanship and design. Let us not forget how it may have taken weeks or months for this plant to grow in order for us to see this beautiful flower. Who caused the rain to fall so that it might grow? Who caused the cycles of life that needed to exist in order for the soil to have the proper nutrients so this flower might bring the fragrance and joy into our life? Jeremiah tells us how God has a plan for our lives. A plan by definition isn't a singular random act that just happens. It infers an organized pattern of events and behaviors that works its way to a desired conclusion. Oftentimes, the blessings we receive today are the results of God being able to use the faithful hands of what others have done in the past in order that He might bless us today. While enjoying the beauty of the moment, let's not fail to stand in awe at all that our God has done in the past to bring this particular moment into our life.

If in our hearts we consider these things and marvel at the depth of love God shows for us in answering even a simple prayer such as this, I believe there is another aspect of God's planning that is by far greater. In the book of Ephesians, Paul wrote, "For he chose us in him before the creation of the world...through Jesus Christ, in accordance with his pleasure and will" (Eph. 1:4–5 NIV). The apostle Peter also wrote in his first letter these words: "It was not with perishable things...you were redeemed...but with the precious blood of Christ...He was chosen before the creation of the world, but was revealed in these last times for your sake" (1 Pet. 1:18–20 NIV).

For too many people, they view the sacrificial death of Jesus Christ on the cross as the final effort of a frustrated God as a means of hopefully reaching a sinful people and bringing them back into relationship with Him. Here, both the apostle Peter and the apostle Paul show us that from before the beginning of time, God's desire and plan was for a restored relationship with those He would create in His image. God knew, before time began, that this restoration would require the sacrificial death and resurrection of his Son. And yet He loved us so much that He still formed us from the earth He had created and breathed breath into our lungs, giving us life. He loved us so much that He gave us the opportunity to choose and know right from wrong. He loved us so much that even while we chose wrong rather than right, He knew that the same ability to choose wrong meant we could and ultimately would choose life and make the choice to love Him and walk with Him, as was His desire from the beginning of time.

If our God loves us so much that He hears the cries of our heart and answers our prayers for even the smallest of things for which we ask, can we even begin to fathom the immenseness and intenseness of His love, knowing that He planned from before our time ever began to draw us toward Him, and love us, and allow us to love Him? All I can say again is, "Thank You, Father!"

MOMENTS FROM THE MOUNTAINSIDE

A Very Present Help

Located in western South Dakota, in the middle of the Black Hills National Forest and the Mount Rushmore National Memorial, is one of this country's great treasures. Millions of people drive up and down the area roadways to come to this place where, some ninety years ago, a man by the name of Gutzon Borglum began to carve out of a granite mountain in this area, a memorial to what many believe to be four of the greatest men who have served in the role of president of the United States. It is here one will be able to view the national landmark called Mount Rushmore. On this mountain you will see the likenesses of presidents George Washington, Thomas Jefferson, Theodore Roosevelt, and Abraham Lincoln. The artist and sculptor, Mr. Borglum, felt that each of these four men had, in their very own way, made a significant and critical contribution to the fabric that went into making the United States of America the country which it is today.

Though there are many ways for one to be able to get to Mount Rushmore, there are three routes that are the most common roads used. The most common route used by visitors and residents alike is to take Highway 16 out of Rapid City, South Dakota, and after making a short drive of just over twenty-three miles (while traveling over Highways 16 and 16a and Highway 244), one is able to pull into the parking garage that is located just a few hundred yards downhill from this monumental carving. Another common route that might be taken is to drive north on Highway 79, and after turning left onto Highway 40, one can follow this road through the foothills of the Black Hills and soon arrive at Mount Rushmore. A third way in which people often are introduced to Mount Rushmore is to drive up the notorious road called Iron Mountain Road from Custer State Park, heading toward the north. Here the traveler will drive up one side of the mountain and down the other through three iconic tunnels, each having their own unique view of Mount Rushmore, driving over three different "pigtail" bridges and driving around one switchback after another in their quest to see the sixty-foot tall carvings that so many love.

However, one of the real joys of visiting this area, and taking the time to see Mount Rushmore, is to try to discover how many different places there are throughout this area where one might be able to see a glimpse of Mount Rushmore. Many are close and personal, such as when you are at the National Park and walking down the Avenue of Flags or standing out on the grand viewing area. A real treat can be had when sitting in the dining room, eating a very enjoyable lunch and seeing the beauty of the monument through the huge glass windows that frame the beauty of the carving. In the town of Keystone, there is another view of the mountain carving from the top of a local hill, after you have taken a chair-lift ride to the top. As you leave the town of Keystone, there is another view you can see. There are also other views visible as you approach the mountain from the Rockerville Road. You can see Mount Rushmore from north of Hermosa on Highway 79 or while on Highway 16 as you leave Rapid City. As you approach Rapid City on Interstate 90 from the east, you can see the monument lit up at night. Heading toward the Badlands National Park on Highway 44, there are multiple places where you can see the nearly white carving as it stands out against the deep-green tree-covered hills of the area. Whether you are standing in front of this sculpture, or you are coming from Keystone, or on the Iron Mountain Road, or on the Rockerville Road, or from Highway 16, Highway 79, Highway 244, or even Highway 40, the beauty and majesty of this mountain carving is very real each time you see it, no matter how different your location is.

As I thought of the way you can see Mount Rushmore from so many vantage points and how it is so evident wherever you are in this portion of the Black Hills of South Dakota, I considered how similar it is to our relationship with our Lord. Sometimes, in the beauty of the day, we may be able to experience His presence as if we were standing right before Him in His presence. Other times, when the road is rough and throws us curves, His presence is not as obvious but nevertheless is still there, standing as majestically as ever. Sometimes we may not even be expecting to see Him or looking for Him, and then when we turn the next corner, He is there just as He has always been. He is there as we look into the eyes of the newborn baby, even as he is in the smile of the person who may have just taken their final breath. Just as one cannot escape the presence of Mount Rushmore as you drive up and down the highways in the Black Hills, one cannot escape the fact that wherever we might go in the pathways of our life, our God and our Savior is there, standing true and tall, etched into the very fabric of all that we call reality. His presence is not in doubt. It is only our view that changes from time to time. In the Bible, the author of the forty-sixth psalm wrote:

> God is our refuge and strength, an ever-present help in trouble. Therefore we will not fear, though the earth give way and the mountains fall into the heart of the sea, though its waters roar and foam and the mountains quake with their surging. There is a river whose streams make glad the city of God, the holy place where the Most High dwells. God is within her, she will not fall; God will help her at break of day. Nations are in uproar, kingdoms fall; he lifts his voice, the earth melts. The LORD Almighty is with us; the God of Jacob is our fortress. (Ps. 46:1–7 NIV)

Even as the national monument that we call Mount Rushmore is an imposing, ever-present sight as one drives on the highways and back roads of the beautiful Black Hills of South Dakota and it is there whether or not we happen to be looking to see it at any given time, our God is ever present in all the journeys we take in life. There are times when He is undoubtedly standing there before us and when we are fully aware of his presence. But there are times when He may be there, looking out for those who call Him Lord, even though our gaze is on other things that have taken our focus off Him. Can we say, as did the psalmist, "The Lord Almighty is with us; the God of Jacob is our fortress"? (Ps. 46:7 NIV). Do we set our sights on trying to find Him at every turn? Perhaps the reason why we don't see His presence is that we are failing to look for it.

From the East to the West

It was a crisp and clear late winter day as we headed westward on Interstate 80 from the area of Des Moines, Iowa. The temperature was just above the freezing mark. The skies were a light blue with a few white puffy clouds hanging here and there, occasionally creating the cooling effect that comes from a shadow as the clouds come between the warmth of the mid-March sun and those on the highways below. By the time we would finish this trip, we would end up over seven hundred miles away, near the eastern edge of the state of Wyoming.

Perhaps what was most notable on this trip today was how, from the one horizon to the other, all a person could see was one cornfield after another. Once planted and harvested, each acre might represent as many as 40,000 ears of corn. Each mile would consist of some 640 acres. Each horizon might be as much as 10 to 15 miles away to both the east and to the west. As I pondered the incredible amount of corn I might drive by once the planting and harvesting seasons were finished, I realized the amount of food that was represented by these fields was of a magnitude I would never be able to comprehend.

Later in the day, during this same journey, we found ourselves driving through the vast prairie lands of South Dakota. Whereas the land we had driven through earlier in Iowa had been covered by corn stalks (towering some nine to ten feet in the air), this land was now covered by seas of gently waving golden-tanned prairie grass, waving gently in the breeze, as if orchestrated by some giant invisible hand moving the air along to the tune of some silent symphony. From one horizon to the other, the prairie grass waved as if giving greeting to those passing by.

As we drew nearer to our final destination, the seas of prairie grass disappeared and the barren rolling hills of dried grasses and scrub brush dominated the view for mile after mile. Even though the nature of the vegetation that now covered this land had changed from the very lush covering of two-foot-tall grasses to the very sparse sprigs of ground-hugging grasses and scrub brush, there was one way in which each changing scene remained true to each of the previous environments that we had passed through. As far as one could see, from horizon to horizon, and for hundreds upon hundreds of miles up and down the highways we drove, the sea of grasses filled the land, the tall cornstalks grew and stretched upward toward the sky, and the rolling hills covered in scrub brush rolled on past the point on the horizon where our eyes could no longer see. Whether it is the view from the deck of the ocean going vessel where the waters that surround you seem to extend up into the very sky, or whether it is when driving throughout the mountains of the eastern and western parts of our country, there is one common truth that I have learned throughout our travels. For one to be able to fully comprehend the immensity of this land we call home is a daunting, if not impossible, task to be able to achieve.

As I considered this day, the tiny and insignificant nature of how I felt as compared to the magnitude of my surroundings, I was reminded of the truth of a verse that the apostle Paul wrote in Ephesians 3:17–19. It is here he wrote:

> And I pray that you, being rooted and established in love, may have power, together with all the saints, to grasp how wide and long and high and deep is the love of Christ, and to know this love that surpasses knowledge—that you may be filled to the measure of all the fullness of God. (Eph. 3:17–19 NIV)

Even though it is right and proper and good to consider and remember the humanity of Jesus our Messiah, and how His life relates to the life that our God calls us to live and has created us for, we must also always remember the fact that "In the beginning, God…" (Gen. 1:1 NIV). While there are times where we will be focused on our lives and all that is going on around us, we must never forget that before time ever existed as we know it, God was and God created. If it makes us feel small and insignificant to consider how all we see in our world is but a minute portion of the entirety of the incredible universe that God created and we are a miniscule part of our world, perhaps that is good. If God created all, then He is creator of all. That is the nature of the one we call our God and our provider.

However, even as we do consider the incredible disproportionality of our existence in relation to that of our God, perhaps we can be comforted in this: the God who made the entire universe and all that is in it (even those far reaches which we cannot see yet) is the same God who loved us so much that His Son died on the cross to pay the price for our sins so that someday we might be able to live in His presence forever. Around three thousand years ago, a man, who rose from being a lowly shepherd, to being the king of his people's land wrote, "For as high as the heavens are above the earth, so great is his love for those who fear him; as far as the east is from the west, so far has he removed our transgressions from us" (Ps. 103:11–12 NIV). Even greater than the views we have of the crops that go from horizon to horizon, and the mountains that reach into the clouds above, and the waters of the ocean that stretch to the edge of our world and beyond is the love that our God has for us. Even greater yet is how far removed from us is the punishment of our sins for which God has forgiven us. God forgives, and then He removes the price for those sins from our account. But first, we must ask.

Have you asked God to forgive you for those sins that you have committed? Do you know the freedom that comes from having the penalty of those sins removed from your shoulders? Would you ask Him today to be your Lord, your Savior, and the answer you have been looking for? Can we pray together?

Gracious Heavenly Father, today we recognize that you and you alone are God. We look to you as the provider and creator of all that we have. We may not understand all that it means, but we recognize that Jesus the Christ is your Son and has already paid the price for my sins.

But first, I need to ask. So, Father, would you forgive me my sins? I have done wrong, and I have saddened your heart, as I know you created me for something far better than what this world has to offer. I accept Jesus as my Lord and Savior, and I desire to walk in relationship with you from today onward, and my hope is to grow and mature in my relationship with you. I accept your forgiveness, and I give you thanks and honor and glory for who you are and for your love and faithfulness. It is this love I desire. In the precious name of Jesus, I ask these things. Amen and Amen...

Tears of a Broken Heart

> The king's command was so urgent and the furnace so hot that the flames of the fire killed the soldiers who took up Shadrach, Meshach and Abednego, and these three men, firmly tied, fell into the blazing furnace. (Dan. 3:22 NIV)

As incredibly beautiful as the scenery has been as we have driven over the highways and roads of this country, there have been at least a few times when our expectations of what would come around the next turn in the highway would be dealt a horrific blow.

One warm fall afternoon, after we had left church for the day, we traveled north from the little town of Interior, South Dakota, on Highway 377, with the hopes of meeting up with Highway 240, which is the main thoroughfare through Badlands National Park. Even though the immediate terrain surrounding Highway 377 is not noteworthy in its own sense, the view of the distant hills and spires of the Badlands is definitely a treat to the eyes. Whereas the lands on each side of Highway 377 are flat, bare, dry sandy soil with only an occasional scrub brush dotting the landscape, the majestic towers and hills of the Badlands rising up from the flat prairie lands below give one the initial impression that perhaps our destination was to some faraway, distant planet. The green of the cedar and pinion trees covered the landscape in small groves at times and in isolated bunches at other times. The wildlife as always was in great abundance. The graceful pronghorn antelope peacefully grazed along the roadside. The eagles and hawks soared overhead. The bighorn sheep rested lazily only feet from the edge of the road. The mighty buffalo basically did whatever they wanted.

Continuing north on Highway 240, after entering the park, you pass trails and pathways where one can hike among the caramel-colored clay-type formations for which this land is noted. You can stop for places with names such as the Window Trailhead and the Notch Trailhead, and even the Castle Trailhead. As you continue on the road that runs through the prairie lands that make up most of the park, you head north toward Interstate 90. This is the path that we took on this day.

As we left the Badlands National Park, the beauty of the views that we had enjoyed ended abruptly as the view before us turned from that of a lush green landscape under a beautiful blue sky to a smoldering mass of charred landscape that would stretch for mile after mile. Perhaps it came from a carelessly discarded cigarette being thrown from the car or perhaps it came from some other source. The result however was the same: over forty thousand acres of blackened and destroyed grasslands and farmlands. Hundreds of livestock had perished due to the racing fire. Buildings were burned and crumbled in a way that only a memory of where they were still existed. Fences were destroyed. Telephone and light poles looked like giant matchsticks, some with holes burned through the very middle of the pole even though the pole still stood. The flames could still be seen attacking any fuel that remained in its path, and the stench of the smoke still hung low in the air.

As we looked at the devastation that lay before us, and in spite of how horrific the scene before us was, our thoughts turned toward those who lived in the path of this firestorm and may have lost everything they owned. What must they be feeling? Shock? Anger? Relief that at least they survived? What will we do now?

In the book of Daniel, the story is told of three men, whose names were Shadrach, Meshach, and Abednego, who also were faced with going through a horrible situation not of their own making. Though the reason for their situation was far different, I believe there is an important lesson we can learn from how these three men endured and survived what they faced.

If you read the story of these three men, as found in the first three chapters of the book of Daniel, you will see that whenever Shadrach is mentioned, so is Meshach and Abednego. Whenever Meshach is mentioned, so also is Shadrach and Abednego. Likewise, Abednego is never mentioned apart from Shadrach and Meshach. So evident is the linking of these three men together that in these three chapters alone, this grouping is mentioned some thirty-six times. Shadrach, Meshach, and Abednego were taken in captivity together. They studied and were taught together. They lived together, and they served together. As well, they were even sent to what should have been their deaths together. In the most difficult time of their lives, Shadrach, Meshach, and Abednego were able to find the strength they would need to endure the most difficult experience they would ever face. When we are faced with going through the horrific evils that we might find ourselves facing, one of the greatest sources of strength we will find is in wrapping ourselves in those relationships that we have built together throughout the prior years of our lives.

There is a second source of strength though that we cannot overlook. In chapter 3, it is written that King Nebuchadnezzar said, "Look! I see four men walking around in the fire…and the fourth looks like a son of the gods" (Dan. 3:25 NIV). When Shadrach, Meshach, and Abednego found themselves in the midst of what should have destroyed them, God met them where they were. He didn't remove them from the trial. He also didn't abandon them. Jesus told us, as it is written in Matthew, "Lo, I am with you always, even unto the end of the world" (Matt. 28:20 NIV). Shadrach, Meshach, and Abednego had faithfully followed in the faith of their fathers as they remained faithful in their relationship to their God. God remained faithful to His promise as He met these three Hebrew men and walked them through their needs.

Do you have a need today that can only be met by God as He desires to make His presence known in your life? Even as you remain faithful in your relationship with Him, He will remain faithful to His word and to you.

Gracious Father, there are incredible hurts and pains that we all will go through and must endure. We don't understand any reason why, but we know that somehow, through this, you can be glorified. Would you help us to be faithful to you as we pray you will be to us. We will give you the glory and the honor that only you deserve. In Jesus's name, Amen.

The Glories of His Majesty

The late fall sun had broken over the eastern horizon just a few hours earlier, and the highway leading out of town to the west was still covered with slush and ice from the nearly foot of freshly fallen snow of the last few days. As the truck headed up over the first pass that I would travel through this day, the sky was a bright, beautiful blue before me. The sun from behind me glistened off the freshly fallen snow that covered the hillsides and fields of my journey. The dark greens of the evergreen trees and bushes stood in contrast with the golden grasses that were waving in the breeze and with the skin-colored tans of the leaves on the trees that lined the fields and hills along the road. As we descended down the western slope of the pass, the ebony black of the coal piles lay juxtaposed to the wisps of snow that covered them like a blanket and with the grays and browns of the long-ago abandoned buildings and structures created by their previous residents.

As my senses took in the virtual feast of all the beauty that surrounded me, I couldn't help but be drawn to the verse that the apostle John wrote in his gospel, as found in chapter 21, verse 25, where he wrote, "Jesus did many other things as well. If every one of them were written down, I suppose that even the whole world would not have room for the books that would be written" (John 21:25 NIV).

Each mile I drove there was a new example of beauty to behold. Perhaps it might be the river to my left meandering through the valley. Or perhaps it might be the coyote running across the grasslands trying to distance itself from the road and the inherent dangers that it might bring. I was treated to varying views of the lava stone walls, dependent upon whether the sun was hidden behind one of the clouds blowing through or whether the sun broke free from the restraints of the clouds that had come between it and the wonders of God's creation that surrounded me on all sides. To be able to capture all the examples of beauty before me would prove to be a task that would be impossible to do.

As Christians, do we likewise fail to take in the incredible and unending beauty of the total nature of whom our Lord and God is? Even with all that God's Word tells us about the faithfulness, goodness, and love of our God, John tells us there wouldn't be enough room in the entire world to write about all that Jesus did while He walked with man here on earth. Have we become so entrenched in the typical and traditional aspects of our relationship with our Lord that we miss seeing some of the extraordinary acts of beauty and love that he has committed? Are we being too busy looking down the highway of life, worrying only about what might come around another curve? Do we miss seeing the young doe and her fawn lazily feeding in the field to our left? Is our picture of the drive we are on diminished because we haven't taken the time to see the beaver lodge that rose from the edge of the pond and which is a witness of the life existing there, even though that life may not be able to be seen by our eyes? Each detail that we miss of the valley that we are driving through is much the same as missing out on the details of the wonderful beauty and fullness of whom our Lord is. Sometimes I fear we fail to comprehend what Matthew meant when he wrote that we need to "Love the Lord your God with all your heart, and with all your soul and with all your mind" (Matt. 22:37 NIV). Too often we are content to just get from point A to point B and are thus content to drive the road we are on, as if our vision is tunnel bound, looking only for the light at the end of the tunnel.

Father, would you open our eyes today so we might be able to fully see the glories of your majesty? Would You help us to see that even the smallest of sparrows sitting and singing on the tree branch above can be a blessing from You as we scurry along below? Father, may we seek to glorify and honor You as we try to recognize Your handiwork in even the smallest, seemingly most insignificant aspects of our life, knowing it is in those quiet corners of our lives that Your love sometimes is the most evident! Holy Father, we honor You today!

Change of Plans

There are some times when life throws us a curve. We make our plans. We study and research every aspect that we need to study. We organize every aspect of our life so that we are chugging along the tracks of life in pursuit of the end goal that we have sought, and then life throws that curveball at us, and we feel like we are heading back to the dugout. Things aren't always what we thought they would be. And so it seemed to be on this beautiful fall day as we turned off Interstate 64 and headed toward a little town of Stanton, Kentucky.

In our travels, we had driven through this particular section of Kentucky on more than one occasion. The beautiful rolling hills of Kentucky, which were covered with every imaginable color of green, reminded one of the waves of an ocean during a summer sailing through a storm. The hills as great moving waves rising up on one side of the road and then the other. The surveyors (who long ago had laid out the path our journeys now took) laid out their course to take advantage of the valleys when they could but then around the next curve tunneled through the limestone and shale base of the hill in front of them. Through each curve we took and each valley we drove, we enjoyed the incredible beauty that nature had for us to view as we looked far out to the horizon to absorb God's beauty like a sponge does in a glass of water.

This day was different though. As we left the comfort of the wide ribbons of the interstate, we entered the narrow, winding corridors of the hairpin curves so aptly named. The umbrella formed by the trees overhead was created by decades of trees and vines growing together and providing the shade one encounters along the twisting, turning, rising, and falling narrow roadways of this part of the state.

The tree-covered bluffs; the small underground springs bubbling up from the ground beneath; the occasional squirrel seen racing up and down the overhead tree branches; the herd of deer one would see in the sunlit meadows that occasionally popped into view; the flock of wild turkeys running in and out of the deep, thick undergrowth below all added to the peace and tranquility of what we would enjoy.

Over three thousand years ago, a young man by the name of Jonathan encountered a situation that he had never expected before. The differences of what would normally be expected and what was in reality were stark. From the safety of the rocks in which he hid, Jonathan stepped forward and said to his armor-bearer, "Come, let's go… Perhaps the Lord will act in our behalf. Nothing can hinder the Lord from saving, whether by many or by few" (1 Sam. 14:6 NIV). And Jonathan went. And his armor-bearer went. And God provided.

Sometimes we spend our whole lives planning on what and where we plan on going, only to have God send us down a different path than what we ever thought of or planned for. Our original plan wasn't wrong. However, when God can send us down a path where we have to leave our comfort zone and travel to places where we have to trust and rely on Him (being as we know we can't do what needs to be done in our own strength), God calls us to do something which brings *Him* praise and glory and honor. When we can testify of our inabilities, others will be able to see God's abilities. Perhaps John the Baptist said it best, when he said in John 3:30, "He must become greater; I must become less" (NIV). Are you willing to step out from the comfort and security of your plans so that others might see who your Jesus is? Are you willing today to allow others the opportunity to give glory to God, even if it means you receive none? Are you willing to allow your God to be God of all?

In the Eye of the Beholder

One of the joys of traveling together as a family or a group is seeing the many different aspects of our surroundings that grab the attention of the people you are with.

As we set out for our drive this day, we knew we were heading into territory that would be new and different from anything we had ever seen before. Behind us lay the comfort and security of where we had been and where we had stayed. Ahead of us lay the unknown. For some in the group, the opportunity today to be able to see the mountains that are ahead was the fulfillment of a life's dream. For others, today was nothing more than a necessary evil and an opportunity to get from place A to place B in the fastest time possible. For each person in the vehicle today, beauty would come with its own definition.

There are those for whom a drive through the mountains is one of the most beautiful experiences they can imagine. For these individuals, it might be the deep-blue-and-gray coloration of the mountain peaks covered with their pure-white snowcaps and that rise far up into the azure-blue skies like majestic cathedrals of worship that captures a person's awe. Or perhaps it is the crisp, clean air of which they can take deep breaths in from these higher altitudes that draws their affection. Then there are those who might be drawn to the mountain drive solely for the anticipation of coming across the hidden valleys they hope to find. Here, with their thick green carpets of grass and wild flowers, one might catch a glimpse of the herds of elk or deer that come down out of the forests above to eat, or a herd of the massive beast called the buffalo as it grazes lazily on the grass before it, or may even of a mountain pond teaming with flocks of geese and ducks taking a brief repose from their migratory flights.

For others, whose heritage might have included more of a Midwestern flair, driving past the miles and miles of the tall green corn and bean fields might be the most relaxing of sights as it reminds them of the home they grew up in so many years ago.

Still for others, there might not be anything more beautiful than being able to sit on a postcard-perfect white sandy beach with the warmth of the waves gently slapping near their feet, watching as the sun slowly sets in the west, turning the sky to every imaginable shade of orange and red as it appears to slowly slip beneath the water's edge.

I have known some that find the beauty of the city to be what warms and comforts them the most. Perhaps it is there that they grew up. Where others might see a city as being chaotic and turbulent in nature, these individuals might see the hustle of the city as a place of opportunity and excitement. It is here in the city where their favorite sports team may play. Perhaps in their city is a favorite museum or zoo or gallery. It is in the chaos of the city where one might see the flurry of activity that surrounds them as being a picture of a well-oiled piece of machinery, whirring and buzzing about them just like the many pieces of the inner workings of a grandfather clock.

In these many ways, I have come to recognize the true meaning of the phrase, "Beauty is in the eye of the beholder" (*Molly Bawn*, Hungerford, M. W., 1878). For each of the scenes above, there are people who might find them to be the ultimate picture of beauty. For every person who loves the majestic beauty of the mountain, there is a person who loves the beauty of the flat nearly inhospitable high desert climate. Here, you will find the blooming of the desert cacti in the spring and the uniqueness of each form of vegetation, whether it is the lowly prickly pear cactus; or the giant saguaro cactus with its multiple arms stretching high in the sky; or even the Joshua Tree, looking as if it is holding a spear in hand, ready for battle. For each, the recognition of beauty is determined by the one who stands before it and derives joy from being in its presence.

With this in mind, how then should we understand the verses that Solomon wrote in the book of Ecclesiastes? Here he wrote:

> He has made everything beautiful in its time. He has also set eternity in the hearts of men; yet they cannot fathom what God has done from beginning to end...I know that everything God does will endure forever; nothing can be added to it and nothing taken from it. God does it so that men will revere him. (Eccles. 3:11, 14 NIV)

Another verse that we need to consider is found in Genesis, where it says, "So God created man in his own image, in the image of God he created him; male and female he created them" (Gen. 1:27 NIV).

Doesn't it mean then that it would be rightful and proper to accept that *if* we were created by God and that *if* everything He has made He sees as being beautiful, then our God, the Creator God of all the universe, looks and sees us as being beautiful to *Him*? What warmth that should bring to our hearts and lives! Even as the sight of the mountains above, or the sands along the sea shore, or even the fields of the plains bring joy and excitement to those who find them beautiful, our Father above finds joy and excitement as He looks to us.

There are times in our lives when the last thing we might feel about ourselves is that we are anything close to being described as being beautiful. But God sees us that way! There are times when all those around us may look at us as the last player they would want on their team. But God created us in His image, and He sees us as being beautiful. There are maybe even times when we may want to question our very worth. But Solomon wrote that God created us beautiful in His eyes and for all eternity. Even as we work hard and may sacrificially give up other things just so we can go to and do those things that we believe bring beauty and joy into our lives, we are what brings joy and beauty into the eyes of our Father, our

Creator. Where others see our faults and sins, God sees His creation and sees it as being beautiful and good.

If in the eye of our Lord and God we are seen as something that brings joy to Him and represents the beauty of His workmanship, how can we see anything less?

Bumps and Bruises

Today was my day to make a drive up the road that has been given the name of the Highway of Legends. The Highway of Legends winds slowly through the Purgatoire Valley of south central Colorado, where it starts in the small historical town of Trinidad, Colorado. As it curves and climbs to the west and north, it makes its way through towns with names that reveal so much about its heritage such as Cokedale, Primero, Segundo, Weston, and Stonewall. It continues onward and upward as it goes past the beautiful lakes of the area that provide the drinking water for the town of Trinidad, which is now some thirty miles away. It continues past the lush green meadows, the heavy forests of the evergreens that cover most of these hillsides, and the many aspens interspersed among the pines with their ivory-white bark accentuated with the black dots where branches had once grown. The Highway of Legends rises nearly four thousand feet before cresting at the top of Cucharas Pass, where it then begins its descent down to the town of LaVeta, Colorado, and Highway 160, which takes the traveler back to Walsenburg and Interstate 25.

As I was driving along Highway 12 today, enjoying the cold winter beauty of a freshly fallen snow, I couldn't help but notice the many well-aged and often dilapidated buildings that line this particular highway. There were several churches, and there were many barns and outbuildings. There were grocery stores where people from past generations might have come to buy their needed supplies. Along this road, you might also see one of the many run-down, broken-down, dilapidated buildings where a person or group of people may have lived many years ago.

As I looked at this one building in particular, I couldn't help but wonder who had lived there and how long ago it had been. Does this building go back to the time when over one hundred years ago, coal mining was so prevalent in this area? How many people might have lived in this house? At only perhaps eight-by-ten feet in size, by today's standard, it is barely big enough to be considered a shed. However, a few generations ago, this structure may have been home to an immigrant family who had come to this area so that the father might try to provide for his family of maybe six, seven, or eight children. With the roof in such a state of disrepair and no visible evidence of a chimney, I wonder if there was even a fireplace with which this family was able to stay warm in the cold, wet winters that are experienced here in Southern Colorado.

When I looked at these buildings from this perspective, they became so much more than just a run-down, falling-apart, dilapidated compilation of building materials. These buildings became a piece of the living history of the lives that were once lived here, building this society and culture we now enjoy.

I have to wonder what would happen though if we took as much time in the church (or even in our interpersonal relationships) to give as much consideration to each other as we look at the broken-down faces and hands of those we meet, which often bear the scars of battles and troubled days. Oftentimes we want to yell at each other to forget those things that are in your past and move on, drawing on the verses written by Paul in Philippians 3:12–14 where he wrote:

> Not that I have already obtained all this, or have already been made perfect, but I press on to take hold of that for which Christ Jesus took hold of me. Brothers, I do not consider myself yet to have taken hold of it. But one thing I do: Forgetting what is behind and straining toward what is ahead, I press on toward the goal to win the prize for which God has called me heavenward in Christ Jesus. (NIV)

However, we must also remember the many times in Scripture we are told to "remember" our past. Sometimes the past we recall can rightly be called a pit. This pit can be a description of a physical place. This is what Joseph was thrown into, as told about in Genesis 37:24. Many times, the pit we are told to consider represents a place where evil exists, such as what John wrote about in Revelation 9:2. Let's remember though that the pit can also be a place of positive reinforcement, such as what Isaiah wrote about in verse 51:1 of his book. Isaiah calls us to "listen to me, you who pursue righteousness and who seek the LORD: Look to the rock from which you were cut and to the quarry from which you were hewn" (NIV). Here, Isaiah is reminding those to whom he is speaking of the nature of their past. The Children of Israel were being challenged to remember that the God they served was the same God their father Abraham had served. Over twenty times in the Old Testament alone, God's word repeats the phrase in some manner "Abraham, Isaac, and Jacob" (Deut. 1:8 NIV). They were told to remember that the rock from which they were cut came from is the same stock and quarry as did the rock of their forefathers Abraham and Isaac and Jacob and Moses.

Let's not be discouraged as we look at the bumps and bruises that we receive along our life's path. But let us, as even did Moses, as did Isaiah, as did the apostle Paul, and as did the apostle John, consider those well-worn timbers and planks that hold together our structures as reminders of the faithfulness of the one whom we call our Father and our Messiah. Let's remember that each one of the cracks or chips in the façade that we try to hide from others represents a battle that we went through and in which God gave us the victory. Let's remember that the building that has no dents, dings, or scratches in it has most likely never been used. The scars we focus on in our own lives, and in the lives of others, are maybe not as much scars as they are battle ribbons and awards from the One we serve.

God's Timing

If a person were to ever spend much time driving through the hills and valleys of the upper Black Hills in western South Dakota, it is more than likely that they would end up driving down a short piece of highway that goes by the name of Alt 14. This relatively short piece of roadway is only about twenty miles long and is built upon what was, until the 1930s, the bed of a railroad line that traversed this path. Today, Alt 14 is the roadway that takes tourists, business people, and local residents alike through what is labeled by some as one of the most beautiful roadways in the world. This roadway is the path that takes you through beautiful Spearfish Canyon.

It was on a late fall day when we decided to drive through the canyon. Earlier that day, we had traveled through the high plains that led us down to the town of Spearfish, South Dakota. Knowing we had nothing pressing that day, and that each day driving the canyon is as different of an experience as was the day before, we made the easy choice to take this short out-of-the-way drive as we headed to get to towns of Deadwood and Lead, South Dakota.

As we left home, the skies were overcast but there was no precipitation. By the time we arrived in Spearfish, a light misting rain began to fall. As we got ready to leave Spearfish, the mist began to turn to snow. Now, as we made the turn onto Alt 14, to head south into the Canyon, the snow began to fall in earnest. What was showing just an hour earlier as the deeply colored greens of the ponderosa pines and the yellow of the limestone bluffs with the occasional white barks of the aspens and birch trees of the valley was already becoming laden with the fresh snowfall of the day. With little wind and equally as little sunshine, the snow began to accumulate. Seeing how quickly the snow built up on the road, one could easily understand how cold the temperatures in the valley must have been as of late. Occasionally, one could see the ice already beginning to build up on the trees and boulders that had fallen and now lay across Spearfish Creek that runs parallel the length of the canyon. The occasional pond that was formed by one of the several small dams that had been constructed along the creek rightfully earned the distinction of being considered a reflection pond. It was in this environment that I found myself on this day, standing in the subfreezing temperatures of the day, snow falling increasingly heavier on the snow-covered roadway with little sun to be found, trying to take pictures on my cell phone, which I dreamt might be competitive with those pictures taken by a professional with equipment much more expensive than what I had. It was then that the ah-ha! moment came.

In the Bible, there is a verse found in Jeremiah 29:11, where it is written, "For I know the plans I have for you...plans to prosper you and not to harm you, plans to give you hope and a future" (NIV). Throughout the ages, there have been countless men and women who have clung to that verse in their times of difficulties when they needed a reassurance that God has indeed not forgotten them or forsaken them. As Christ followers, we often find ourselves seeking to find some sort of comfort in our situation when all the troubles we fear seem to be piling up high upon our plate. As I gave consideration to this verse, this canyon, on this day, reminded me of the truths of that promise of God to Jeremiah.

At times, we want to be able to stand before the beautiful reflection ponds that God brings across our path. We love to feel the gentle breeze of the air that softly bends the pine boughs of the trees while gently allowing the snow to softly fall from the sky. We love to hear the rippling of the rapids giving off their reassuring and comforting music that is made from the streams of water cascading down over the boulders and valleys in our life. There is nothing more beautiful than the purity of the freshly fallen white snow sitting on the tree branches and boulders that we have driven around. We love to see the beauty of the reflection pond, where the tree that grows upward to the heavens above now appears to be aiming to the earth below. Even the cool, crispness of the late fall air can be refreshing when compared to the hot, humid days of the summer that was left behind. As these things are all considered in the context of where we find ourselves standing, the reality of God's Word is made clear.

Have we given consideration to the fact that nearly a century earlier, a great number of men sweat and toiled under the heat of the sun to build the railroad bed that this road now rests upon? Have we given consideration to the reality that without the annual freezing and thawing of the winter precipitation, many of these boulders may never have fallen down into this creek? Adding to that, the countless trees and branches that have had to fall throughout the years, and one better understands what it took in order for this creek to be formed in the way it has. Have we given consideration to the fact that without the subfreezing temperatures, we would not be able to enjoy the beauty of the freshly fallen snow? Have we given consideration to the fact that it is due to the heating rays of the summer suns, the moisture in area lakes and streams have evaporated and is now able to fall from the sky where we now stand? Have we given consideration to the fact that today, due to the lack of wind in the canyon, the waters now stand still, allowing one to enjoy the beauty of the reflection of all that is above it?

So then on this day, because of the sweat and toils of others, because of the years of freezing and thawing, because of the freezing temperatures of the day, because of the lack of wind, and because of even the heat and intense suns of the prior summer, we are now able to stand before this incredibly beautiful scene that our God has painted for us. My friends, a journey is not only about where you started and then where you have ended up, it is about all that happens to get us from point A to point B. It is about the struggles that we have had to go through along the way. It is about the impact that others have had on our lives and journeys. It is about what happened yesterday as well as what is happening today. These things are all the things that make up our pathway in life, and even the journey or plan that God has for us.

Perspectives

Driving south on Highway 83 this evening, I found myself in the midst of the beautiful sand hills of North Central Nebraska. The sand hills of this area cover an area of several hundred square miles and lie as a great barrier between the states of South Dakota to the north and Nebraska to the south. For mile after mile, you encounter one rolling hill after another. The difference in height between the tops of many of the hills above and the valleys below may only be twenty to thirty feet at times. Contrasting with the sandy-brown color of the hills is the deep green of the scrub brush that sparsely covers this land. Occasionally, as one drives along the roads of this area and comes over the crest of the hill they have climbed, one might find a beautiful reed-filled lake below. Dependent upon which time of the year you might be traveling, the lake may be covered with the migratory waterfowl that annually will pass this way as they travel to the south in the fall or back to the north in the spring. The beautiful mule deer are a constant sight along this road, as are the many smaller animals that call the sand hills of Nebraska their home.

The time was about six o'clock in the evening, about a half hour before sunset. Just three hours earlier, I had departed south central South Dakota, and before this trip would be over, this truck would be stopping in southern Colorado. For many, this drive might be described as being boring at best. However, the treat that was to be mine tonight would be life-changing. As I gazed out the driver's window, the prairie grasslands were illuminated by the glow of the late afternoon sun. Because of this glow, the grasses of the Nebraska sand hills appeared to be a sea of waving white tassels being briskly blown by the breeze that was moving over the land. Though there were many times this trip had been made when the land was covered white with snow, tonight, not a speck of snow could be seen. It was only the tops of the blowing grasses that appeared to be covered in white. Curious as to whether this was a different type of crop or vegetation than what I had seen before, I gazed over to my right, toward the direction of the setting sun. To the west of my vehicle were the usual browns and tans of the dried-out prairie lands of which I was so familiar. Looking to the left, waves of white blowing in the wind. Looking to my right, dried barren wasteland.

As I thought about the scene that I was looking upon this night, I couldn't help but consider the way in which Jesus consistently looked at the people who might have come across His path. When the teachers and Pharisees of Jesus's day brought a woman to Jesus whom they claimed to have caught in the act of adultery, these leaders, who opposed all that Jesus stood for, looked at this woman as a disposable or wasted entity. However, through the eyes of Jesus, as He considered that she was a person He himself had created in the image of God, He had compassion for her as He said, "Has no one condemned you? Then neither do I condemn you…Go and leave your life of sin" (John 8:10–11).

Likewise, in Luke, we are told of an encounter that Jesus had with a group of men who had leprosy. These men knew what it was like to be outcasts in the cities and towns of which they lived. They were required to announce to all whom they approached that they were afflicted with this disease. To the world around them, they were to be isolated and rejected. Yet, when the path that Jesus the Christ took collided with the path that this group was taking, instead of rejecting this group of men as being a wasted and barren segment of society, He showed love and compassion to them. "When he saw them, he said, 'Go, show yourselves to the priests.' And as they went, they were cleansed" (Luke 17:14 NIV). When the very Son of God chooses to look past the sins and difficulties that were unquestionable in the lives of those whom He met, how can we do any less?

As I considered again the sight that now was before me, I was made aware again how God's heart and desire is for men and women to be redeemed and come back to a saving relationship with Him.

However, when I look away from the Son's (sun's) perspective, I see barrenness and wasteland. Is the reason why we fail to have a heart and a longing for lost souls because we fail to look at them from the perspective of a Son who loved them enough that He willingly went to the cross to die for them, even as He did for us? Have we lost the Son's perspective and have chosen instead to look the other way, viewing the same situation as hopeless and lost and wasted? Have we lost our perspective? We know what His perspective is: "Do you not say, 'Four months more and then the harvest?' I tell you, open your eyes and look at the fields! They are ripe for harvest…!" (John 4:35 NIV). What perspective is ours?

Holding on Tightly

Heading out for a drive today, we knew it was going to be a momentous occasion. From the south, we were approaching the town of Buena Vista, Colorado. The sky today was partly cloudy, with the beautiful blue color of the sky being broken up with an occasional white puffy cloud floating lazily by and a few sparsely located rain clouds with their battleship gray underneath, and the rain visibly drifting down toward the earth as if by the hands of a giant showerhead watering that parcel of land directly below. The road we were on was Highway 285 and is known for the way in which it parallels a range of mountains made up of many of the "14ners" of the state of Colorado. These mountains include names such as Mount Harvard, Mount Yale, Mount Princeton, Mount Oxford, and Mount Columbia. Thus, one can see how this particular portion of the Sawatch Mountain range was given the name of the Collegiate Peaks. Upon leaving Buena Vista on Highway 24 to the north, we continued to see mountains adorned with the most beautiful of robes colored in the reds and yellows and oranges and greens of the fall foliage that covered their hillsides. Above the tree lines of these monstrous creations, one could still see the stark contrast of the patches of cold white snow that inhabited the crevices and ravines of the mountains since falling there last winter.

Soon, we would be making the turn onto Highway 82 at a place called Twin Lakes, where we would begin making our accent up to Independence Pass with its altitude of 12,093 feet. Even though our focus before had been on the beautiful fall foliage of the Collegiate Peaks, here, our attention began to shift focus to the beautiful lakes and streams of the area. Whether it was in the lakes below, such as the Twin Lakes, or the rushing streams heading down from the rains and snowpack of the peaks above, or even whether it was to be seen in the many waterfalls of the area (some of which might have only been a foot or two tall), the water was clear, fresh, and cold. Where the streams would widen out to form one of many ponds, it was not difficult to envision how the deer and wildlife of the area might come to drink of its refreshment. Further up in altitude, where the blankets of trees began to thin and the high-altitude tundra could be found, the nature of the streams began to change. Whereas further below, they would be rushing over the rocks and boulders in a steady stream of rapids, higher up in the tundra, they seemed to be more mellow in nature as they appeared to be more like the remnants from a ball of yarn after having been playfully batted about by a baby kitten. Even as we finally arrived at the top of Independence Pass, we were still amazed to find multiple cool, crisp ponds resting lazily at over 12,000 feet yet still beneath the summit of the local peak.

We exited the car, and after a great deal of labored breathing due to the thinness of the air at this altitude, looked back over the road we had just come. The meandering streams were still able to be seen. The patchwork quilt of the most beautiful of reds, greens, golds, and yellow could still be seen covering the mountainsides below. The newly repaved road below looked like a black with yellow striped garter snake, twisting and turning as it made its assent up the more than four thousand feet we had climbed. The sky was still the typical azure blue of Colorado. The gray-bottomed rain clouds with the streaks of gray rain falling to the earth below were still seen in the area, and the fluffy white clouds continued to fill out the painter's palette of this picture.

It was from this vantage point, my thoughts ran to an encounter that we read about in the Bible, which Jesus had with a young man of financial wealth. In this encounter, the young man came to Jesus, and asked, "What must I do to inherit eternal life?" (Mark 10:17 NIV). Jesus responded to this young man, "You know the commandments: 'Do not murder, do not commit adultery, do not steal, do not give false testimony, do not defraud, honor your father and mother'" (Mark 10:19, NIV). The story continues on. He declared, "All these

I have kept since I was a boy." Jesus looked at him and loved him. "One thing you lack," He said. "Go, sell everything you have and give to the poor, and you will have treasure in heaven. Then come, follow me." At this the man's face fell. He went away sad because he had great wealth (Mark 10:20–22 NIV).

All too often, I believe we err in understanding this story by solely focusing on how the rich young man didn't want to sell his belongings in order that he could follow Jesus. Jesus never said his wealth was bad or wrong. However, Jesus understood that for this individual, his lack of willingness to surrender all in order to follow Jesus was best represented in how tightly he held on to this aspect of his life. Even as we did, when we looked back at this vantage point high up in the mountains, I'm sure this man was able to look back at his life and see many wonderful, beautiful aspects of all that made up the years of his existence. He surely was able to see many good and profitable experiences and events that made him the man he was that day. Unfortunately, he also was able to see the grip that his wealth had over his heart and his life.

A prison guard once asked two of Jesus's followers "Sirs, what must I do to be saved?" (Acts 16:30 NIV). Their reply was simply this, "Believe in the Lord Jesus, and you will be saved—you and your household" (Acts 16:31 NIV). Nothing more needed. Nothing less accepted. Even as Jesus gave His ultimate sacrifice by dying for us on the cross at Calvary, He wants nothing less from us. Does that mean we *have* to give it (whatever "it" represents) all away? No, but as Jesus told this young man of many skills and talents, the only thing keeping us from walking in complete relationship with Jesus Christ, our Lord, our Savior, is that "thing" that we are not willing to let go of.

What are *you* holding on to today that keeps you from fully surrendering and following Jesus, the Christ?

Jesus with Skin On

It was a beautiful winter day as we headed west on Highway 34 from the small town of Belle Fourche, South Dakota. The terrain that began as the dried-grass-covered plains of South Dakota slowly gave way to the periodic hills jutting up from the flatlands below. The further west we traveled, the higher the small prairie bumps became, until the deep blackish green of the evergreens began to cover the sides of the rising hilltops. On the flat prairies below, there was little if any snow covering, contrasting the stark white of the snow with the tan of the dead prairie grasses of last year. However, higher up, here in the hills, the innocence of the pure-white snow could increasingly be seen among the branches of the evergreens and the hidden places of the valleys below. As we traveled even further west, the golden yellow of the limestone bluffs completed the spectrum of the rainbow as they competed with the baby-blue hues of the clear sky above and the brick-red ridges rich in oxidation of the iron minerals they contain, and the deep evergreens of the pine trees that lined the path we had undertook, and the brilliant white snow that soon began to cover the lands around us.

Soon, among all the incredible beauty that now surrounded us, the destination of our choice began to come into view. At first, the stone monolith we had come to visit appeared as just a blip on the horizon. The further we drove, the more hillsides we descended, and the more curves we rounded, the closer the road brought us our destination, that which is called Devil's Tower. As we pulled up to the entrance drive to the first national monument for our country, we looked up in awe at the tower that now rose nearly 1,300 feet above us.

Even though the beauty of this mountain might not be disputed by any who see it, the origins of how it came into existence is openly debated. The Native American people of the area attribute its creation to a variety of legends, many of which include children playing and seeking safety from a giant bear. Some look at this monolithic creation and attribute it to millions of years of movement and shaking and development of the earth's surface. Some look at this great stone structure and believe it is most likely a giant ancient petrified tree stump with a one-thousand-foot wide base. Still others look to this monument and see an incredible example of God's love as He created all we have about us as a witness of who He is and a testimony of His great love for us. Dependent upon who you are and the mindset of what has turned you into the person you are today, Devil's Tower has become perhaps as many different things as there are people who will come and stand at its base, trying to absorb the rugged beauty that they see.

In much the same way, the apostle Paul wrote nearly two thousand years ago:

> Though I am free and belong to no one, I have made myself a slave to everyone, to win as many as possible. To the Jews I became like a Jew, to win the Jews. To those under the law I became like one under the law (though I myself am not under the law), so as to win those under the law. To those not having the law I became like one not having the law (though I am not free from God's law but am under Christ's law), so as to win those not having the law. To the weak I became weak, to win the weak. I have become all things to all people so that by all possible means I might save some. (1 Cor. 9:19–22 NIV)

Even though in these verses, the apostle Paul is not bringing into question the origin of our creation, he is seeking to remind us of the reality of the incredible depth of God's love for us. For those who lived during the times the apostle Paul wrote, the realization they were seeking to serve the God who had created the entirety of the universe was well understood. However, as Jesus demonstrated through the life He lived, the Creator God of the universe also wanted to be seen as a loving, caring Father and as a friend and as a brother. In other places, the Bible describes God as our provider, as God the Rock, as God as the everlasting one, and even as the God who sees me, as well as a host of many other names.

In our world today, even as it was in the days of Jesus and the apostle Paul, there are times when we need to realize the incredible, indescribable magnificence of the Creator God of everything we see. Perhaps there is no other way in which we can fully comprehend the truth that He is God and we are not. However, there are also times when the darkness closes in around us, and we may feel so alone and left out in life. During these times, how our heart is warmed when we consider that our God is the God who sees us. There may also be times when we are struggling and unsure of when or where our next meal will come from or how our need might be met. Perhaps here, God is wanting to remind us that we can and, rightfully, should look to Him as God our provider. And when the very core of our existence might currently be in the midst of being shattered, how encouraging is it to know that the God we love and serve wants to be our Rock and Fortress?

The apostle Paul described his willingness in the above verses to be seen by others in whatever way he needed to be seen in order that, through his witness of God's great love for mankind, others might come to a saving relationship with their Creator, their Rock, their Provider, and the One who sees them. The apostle Paul was fully aware of the truth that how the world sees our God and our Father will be filtered through the lenses of the glasses the world sees us through. Yet he was willing to be used by God to be, as the saying goes, "Jesus with skin on" to the world around him in order that God may be able to reclaim a lost people that were created for Him.

Should we aspire to anything less?

Faithfully Stay

Driving northbound along I-25, at about mile marker No. 4 in Colorado, on the west side of the highway is an old run-down church known only as the Morley Mission. The roof is gone. Most of the two side walls are gone, and the back wall has long ago given into the ravages of the winter winds and storms and to that thing we all battle that is called age. In order to see the Morley Mission in its greatest beauty and grandeur, one must be willing to get up early and see it at the first break of light. This is when the sun is just peaking over the horizon to the east, bathing the mission and the surrounding hillside, trees, and ruins in that beautiful golden-hued light that one only sees at the first moment of early morning dawn. This day, as I was driving by the mission, I thought of the many science fiction shows of our day that typically feature some form of, or derivative, of a time travel portal where one could be whisked away to some faraway place or time.

Here, as I looked at the front door of the mission, it was as if I was being beckoned to its grand and glorious doorway to be somehow raptured away to some other world or existence far from the daily grind and problems that we all normally have to label as life. To be certain, there is a certain truth or element of the Christian experience where we are blessed with being able to be removed and distanced from the problems of life when we are in our restored relationship with our Heavenly Father. In Psalms 23, David wrote about walking through the valley of death. He was not being kept in it. Moses led the children of Israel away from the bondage and captivity of ancient Egypt. Abraham led Lot away from the destruction of Sodom and Gomorrah. Daniel was released from the lion's den.

Even in the Hebrew language of the Bible, one of the names for God is that of a "deliverer." However, as Christians, we must not seek to see the restoring, saving grace of our Father as an escape mechanism from the cruel, crushing blows of the world. In looking at the entirety of the message of God's Word, one is able to find as many times when God called His children to "wait" with Him during those dark and very dangerous times of life. In the book of Matthew, we find it written:

> He took Peter and the two sons of Zebedee along with him, and he began to be sorrowful and troubled. Then he said to them, "My soul is overwhelmed with sorrow to the point of death. Stay here and keep watch with me." Going a little farther, he fell with his face to the ground and prayed, "My Father, if it is possible, may this cup be taken from me. Yet not as I will, but as you will." Then he returned to his disciples and found them sleeping. "Couldn't you men keep watch with me for one hour?" he asked Peter. "Watch and pray so that you will not fall into temptation. The spirit is willing, but the flesh is weak." (Matt. 26:37–41 NIV)

Will our Father, the one who has given so much for us, be able to find us faithful when He needs us to wait? Can we stay in the Garden with Him when He asks us to, even though it may mean our lives are endangered? Am I willing to say, even as Jesus did, "Not as I will, but as you will"? (Matt. 26:39 NIV). Our prosperity message that we preach must always be anchored in the richness of staying in His presence and not in what He might give or provide for our pleasure.

Dear God, if nothing else is accomplished today, may You find me faithful today.

Choices

For any person whose love and joy can be found driving up and down the highways of this country, making choices is an accepted necessity. Where do we want to go today? Do we want to take a drive up into the mountains, where we can be close and intimate with the beauty of God's creation? Maybe we can see the huge herds of majestic elk that have come down into the valleys to feed or the graceful deer that lazily feed at the fencerows and fields that we will pass. Perhaps we will be able to stand and listen to the babbling brook of crystal clear water that has worked its way down from the very tops of the snowcapped mountains above to the lush green valleys below. Will the leaves of the aspens be the light lime-green color of the springtime, which is evidence of the newness of life, that is racing to the skies above after the cold, freezing temperatures of the winter? Or have they begun to turn to the beautiful sun-glow yellow of the fall as they prepare to drop their leaves in anticipation of the long, cold winter that will soon be coming?

Perhaps we might want to take a drive out into the prairies of our lands where we are able to witness the two-foot-tall prairie grasses waving ever so gentle in the warm breezes of the day? Will they appear again today, as if they are a part of that giant ocean of tan-and-white tassels moving in unison, being directed by the hands of the invisible Conductor who seeks to bring all things together into that perfect harmony? In the prairies, we might see the great cities of the lowly prairie dogs, which at one time was said to have covered much of the expanse of all that we call the West. At times, the lonely coyote might be seen racing across the prairies, always looking to where it had just come from, ever mindful of the dangers of being caught out in the open views made possible by the never-ending field of sight of the flat prairielands it calls home.

Maybe we would rather take a drive through the fields of crops that are the source of food and nourishment for so many of the people in our country. So incredible are the miles upon miles where one can drive past the fields of some of the tallest, most productive corn, soybeans, wheat, and hay that has ever been produced. For most, if not all, it may be incomprehensible to fathom the magnitude of the amount of food and crops represented by the millions of square miles of these crops that are created by adding the puzzle pieces of each individual field together to paint the overall masterpiece.

No matter which direction our travels take us, there will always be a series of choices that we will need to make in order for us to have ended our day with the journey of our desires being completed in the manner of our hopes.

It is in much the same way in the Christian life that we find ourselves constantly needing to make choices. As we awake in the morning, we make choices about what our priorities for the day will be. We choose what we will wear for the day and what and where we will eat. We choose where and if we will go to work today. We choose with whom it will be that we associate during the day. We choose where and when we will go to the place we call home at the end of the day. All of what we know to be what we call life is made up and determined by those choices we make on a regular, daily basis.

Over three thousand years ago, there was a man by the name of Joshua who also understood the importance and the necessity of having to make decisions. He recognized that what he did in life and where he went was directly dependent upon the choices he made. He alone was responsible for those choices and recognized that they would determine the direction of his life.

In the book of Joshua, we read where, as Joshua was nearing the end of his life, he said these words:

> But if serving the LORD seems undesirable to
> you, then choose for yourselves this day whom
> you will serve, whether the gods your ancestors

served beyond the Euphrates, or the gods of the
Amorites, in whose land you are living. But as for
me and my household, we will serve the LORD.
(Josh. 24:15 NIV)

As Joshua addressed the Children of Israel, he reminded them
that it would be up to them to decide whether or not they would
continue to serve the God of their fathers: of Abraham, Isaac, Jacob,
and Moses. If they made the choice to not serve the God of their
fathers (the one who had brought them from captivity into posses-
sion of their promised land), then they would be choosing to worship
the gods of their enemies, the ones whose land God had delivered
them from and brought them through. Joshua pointed out to those
around him that, although by this time he was well up in age and
nearing the final days of his life, he was still continuing to make the
choice to serve the God of his forefathers, the same God whom he
had served all his life.

It is in these verses Joshua reminds us that even today, serving
God is not something that comes by accident or is something that
we just grow into but is a conscious decision that we must make. By
so doing, Joshua is being faithful to what his predecessor and mentor
Moses wrote in the book of Deuteronomy, where he said:

This day I call heaven and earth as witnesses
against you that I have set before you life and
death, blessings and curses. Now choose life, so
that you and your children may live and that you
may love the Lord your God... (Deut. 30:19–20
NIV)

What is the choice we will make today? Will we choose to serve
the God who has faithfully guided and directed our paths toward Him?
Will we choose the path of life and blessings? Will we make the conscious decision to say, just as Joshua did and as have the millions who
have followed after him, "We will serve the Lord"? (Josh. 24:25 NIV)

Heavenly Father, may we always choose life!

Perseverance

It was a beautiful, clear spring day when we decided to take a drive up through this nearby canyon. Even though we had been there many times before, we recognized this particular place as one of our go-to places for a brief respite from the sometimes chaotic nature of our everyday lives. Sometimes we might drive this road, just to be able to see the new growth of fresh buds on the trees during the spring. At other times, we might make this journey so we can witness the annual changing of the leaves in the fall. Then there were times we made this trip when our only goal was to make it to the end of the canyon road to the little mom-and-pop restaurant where we could enjoy a lunch, feasting on one of their fabulous Indian tacos.

This day, the entrance to the canyon was anything but eventful. The lush green grasses of the nearby golf course were well manicured as expected. Even though the riverbed that ran this far toward town was clearly seen, there was nary a drop of water in it. The parking lot where the area hikers and bicyclists would leave their cars and vans was empty, and the summer time traffic had not yet begun to clog this hidden jewel.

Entering the canyon, one could hear the chirping of the birds as each one sang their own particular tune. Occasionally, if one were to watch closely, a brown squirrel could be seen scampering across the grounds until it would leap fearlessly up into a nearby tree, where it might play and scurry along the branches of the tree that it called home. Sporadically, the tiny chipmunks might be seen as they would dart out into the road and back again as the four-wheel monsters would come speeding toward them. Other than the birds of the air and the chipmunks and squirrels and an occasional white-tailed deer seen grazing along in the yards and roadsides, there was little evidence of other wildlife that might be seen while making this canyon drive.

As we traveled along, we could see where the winter waters had already made their run down the canyon and the stream ran clear and crisp where it twisted and turned below the hills and trees above. For mile after mile, we would slowly navigate the meandering curves of this valley road, only seeking to enjoy the pleasures and serenity of our current environment.

There is one spot though that often catches our attention, and we often seem to either slow down and take note or stop completely. It is here where a pair of boulders (both of which are larger than a good-size truck and whose weight would be measured in tons and not pounds) have broken off from the hillside above and crashed down into the stream below. They now rest peacefully in the bottom of the canyon and in the midst of the cool, clear mountain stream, which has rerouted its path to either go around, or under, or through the rocky debris. One can only imagine what it must have been like just a couple decades ago when these boulders first broke off from the hillside above, and after crashing through the trees above, came to rest in their current location.

Even as interesting as is the picture as what these two boulders have created with their destructive beauty, there is one aspect in particular that catches the eye of the one who is carefully examining the totality of the picture before them. There, on these boulders, which have sat in this place for twenty to thirty years, are now trees growing in the midst of some of the cracks and crevices of their surfaces. In the midst of these two giant behemoths of limestone, things that caused massive destruction not too many years ago and destroyed hundreds of trees as they cleared a path thirty-feet wide and hundreds of feet long while they plummeted and rolled to the creek bed below, is evidence of new life beginning. In the cracked faces of these giant boulders, seeds from the trees above have not only landed and imbedded themselves, but they have taken root and are now growing and flourishing—in the most unlikely of places.

I couldn't help but think of the connection that this tree has with what it means to be a follower of Jesus the Christ. For these trees, there was a point in their past when the first small hair-like roots began their journeys downward in search of the moisture that they would need for the sustaining of life. When they first came into contact with this rock, the roots had a choice to make. They could stop exactly where they were at, which would mean their existence as roots would cease and their life would then be finished, or as is the case demonstrated by these trees, they could continue growing while working their way around or through the obstacle ahead of them. It is in this way that the obstacle before them would as such become encapsulated into their very being, even to the point of turning the obstacle into a part of their foundation and strength.

How often do we, as Christians, find ourselves beating our heads against the wall seemingly with all options closed before us and having nowhere to turn? It is at times such as these that God wants us to know, as He did Gideon, "The lord is with you, mighty warrior" (Judg. 6:12 NIV). In his own eyes, Gideon could only see the impossible. He responded by saying, "How can I save Israel? My clan is the weakest in Manasseh, and I am the least in my family" (Judg. 6:15 NIV). Gideon could never envision the possibility that God could use him as God's tool to deliver His people. In spite of his doubt though, Gideon continued to turn to and to listen to God's voice. He may have doubted, but he trusted in the God of his fathers. He may have wondered how God would deliver Israel from the hands of the Midianites, but he continued to listen to and follow the words of the One whom he loved. In all he did, Gideon demonstrated tenacity and perseverance in following the leading of His God. In our eyes and in Gideon's eyes, he might have been the most unlikely of people for God to use that day but God did use him and God delivered. Later on, Gideon's lord went on to tell him the reason why He, the God of Abraham, Isaac, and Jacob, wanted to continue to use the unlikely in order that He might accomplish the impossible. It was so that "Israel may not boast against me that her own strength has saved her" (Judg. 7:2 NIV). The unlikely was used to do the impossible.

Can we be willing to be more like the tender hair-like young root of a tree as it searches for the way around or through the hindrance before it? Even then, as that young root grows and matures while weaving its way through the tiny fissures and cracks of the rock, the tree itself continues to grow and mature as the roots continue to increase in size and strength and the rock begins to crumble beneath the tenacity of those small hair-like extensions of the mighty tree above it.

We must never forget we serve a God who can and does use the unlikely to do the impossible.

Treasures

It is through traveling on the dirt and gravel roads, the back roads of an area, that one is able to discover much of what makes the culture of that area truly unique. Traveling up and down the highways of Florida, one is able to see the sprawling green pastures with beautifully maintained fences where many of the greatest racehorses of all time were bred and raised. One also might be able to see the small family-owned tourist spots, long ago abandoned, which were the norm for the tourist industry in that state. Sights such as these were what made up the heritage of Florida long before the huge mega theme parks of today were built, many which are centered on the development of certain merchandising brands. In Iowa, as one leaves the major highways of the state, one can see the homes and school-houses of a century gone by, no longer meeting the needs of a people, a people who have now moved into the cities of the state where the jobs and employment have all gone. Here in Southern Colorado, when one drives on some of the back roads that course through the valleys and canyons that lay between the never-ending ranges of mountains, one is treated to ghost town after ghost town of civilizations of a century ago but which have since been long abandoned.

Such was the site we witnessed as we drove along CR 40.2 that day as we journeyed westward from the town of Ludlow to the community that lay some twenty or more miles away called Cokedale. Even though it was a mid-January day, the skies were the typically beautiful, exceedingly clear Colorado skies. The temperatures were a warm and comfortable fifty degrees for the day, though the air was moved by a cool, brisk breeze that blew across the snow lying on the northern and the eastern slopes of the hills and valleys. As we left the main road and drove underneath the very narrow and very low rail-road overpass, we were soon treated to some of the sights that we had set out to see that day. Here on the right was the foundation of what must have been a company store for one of the many coal mining communities that lined this particular road. The piles of ebony-black coal reached upwards of a hundred feet into the air, resting alongside one of the many rocky, barren hillsides that lined this particular road. As we traveled further down this road, we came across the ruined foundations of what must have been a row of houses. These houses were but a sample of the homes that these miners and families lived in for those few hours each day when they weren't far underground, digging out this precious fuel source for others to heat their homes and businesses with. As we continued to drive down this road, winding to the right and to the left through the valley created by the now tiny stream flowing to our right, we drove through periods of bright sunlight and through periods of dark, shadowy snow-covered roads. Here on the right was an old weather-worn, dilapidated shed that might have been a home for someone who may have ranched in the valley in the past or may have been a shed used for storing supplies for the winter. Standing just a few yards away was a treat that still may occasionally be seen in this area: a wooden-based windmill. This windmill still stood in defiance of the strength and velocity and direction of the wind that has continued to blow through this valley since before the days when this windmill was built by the hands of the settlers of this land.

As we drove mile after mile that day, past the silent reminders and relics of long-forgotten ages, I was reminded of the words that Jesus spoke in Matthew 6:19–21, when He said:

> Do not store up for yourselves treasures on earth, where moths and rust destroy, and where thieves break in and steal. But store up for yourselves treasures in heaven, where moths and rust do not destroy, and where thieves do not break in and steal. For where your treasure is, there your heart will be also. (NIV)

Here in this hidden valley of our area were these silent testimonies of stores and business, of homes and churches, and of rusted cars and trucks that were the treasures of generations long gone. These treasures now were nothing more than crumbled stones and adobe bricks, collapsed tin-and-cedar-shingled roofs, and rusted metal and broken glass. Treasures that lasted but a century or less.

As we walk in relationship with our God, His word tells us to focus on those treasures that will last far longer, in a realm called heaven, a place we will call home for all eternity. Is what God called treasures represented by the words of the apostle Peter when he wrote, "But you are a chosen people, a royal priesthood, a holy nation, a people belonging to God, that you may declare the praises of him who called you out of darkness into his wonderful light. Once you were not a people, but now you are the people of God" (1 Pet. 2:9–10 NIV)?

Isn't the treasure of God's eyes seen as being that which John wrote about when he said, "For God so loved the world that he gave his one and only Son, that whoever believes in him shall not perish but have eternal life" (John 3:16 NIV)?

The joys of walking in a restored relationship with our Lord and God come from knowing the investments that God has made in us. These investments God also calls us to make in each other and are investments that won't rust, or decay, or crumble in the elements of the world but are investments that can be seen as eternal treasures. These treasures are represented by the very best that God has to offer us through the life and death and resurrection of His son Jesus Christ. Are the treasures that we seek to build also built upon the foundation of the very best that we have to offer?

The Whole World
in His Hands

Whenever we have driven the highways of our country, we have found one thing to be consistent in their construction: the turnout or parking space along the side of the road where one can safely exit their vehicle for any number of reasons. A person doesn't need to drive very far up the narrow, winding roads of a mountain pass before they will see at least one, if not multiple, turnouts where the motorist can stop. For some, these turnouts might serve as an opportunity to look back at where they have come from or where they are going to. For some, turnouts work well to give the slower motorist an opportunity to pull over, to allow speedier motorists from behind to pass by safely, thus allowing the slower driver the opportunity to continue on their way with decreased pressure. There are those who may use the turnouts as a means to answer a phone call or text. There are also those individuals who might need to use a place to pull over in order that they might be able to change drivers. Regardless of the need for or use of the turnout is a part of the highway systems that I imagine nearly every driver has used at some time or another.

Today, our need for the use of a turnout arose from our journey to the top of the largest mesa found in the world. The Grand Mesa in western Colorado is home to over 200 lakes on its 500-square-mile top. It rises to an altitude of over 11,000 feet, some 5,000 feet, above the lands in the valleys before. After spending a day driving along the roads of the park where we were treated to the beautiful foliage of fall wherever we looked and the beauty of some of the many lakes, we knew it was time to head back down to the town below. Knowing there was yet that one picture we were still looking for, we watched to see if we could find that special place along the road where the trees and bushes would open up and reveal the valley below in all its beauty.

We didn't have to travel long before we found the spot that we were looking for.

We slowed the car down and pulled over, crossing the very rough point of transition between the road and the turnout, which is so often the case. Exiting the car, we realized this would be the view we were looking for. The opening was framed perfectly by the white-barked aspen trees on each side of the view. To the right, the gentle rise of the side of the mesa was covered with the lush green bushes and trees that hid the rocky hillside. Straight ahead and below us lay the town of Cedaredge, a town of just more than two thousand people. From this distance and height of three thousand to four thousand feet above the town below, one could readily recognize the streets and buildings of the town. Though one could easily see the trucks and cars scurrying about the town, the local residents were too small to be seen. The bright-green pastures that surround the town and where the livestock grazed and fed were easily recognized. Further out and away from the edge of the town, at a distance of perhaps ten to twenty miles, rose the hills and rocky crags that make up the landscape of this area. Farther away, on the distant horizon, one could make out the San Juan Mountain Range of southwestern Colorado. Even on a hazy day such as this, one could easily make out the snow-covered shapes and peaks of this range, which is over one hundred miles away. One can only imagine what it must be like to see this view on a clear, sunny day with no haze to be seen.

Looking out in awe from this vantage point, I had to wonder if this was anything like the encounter Jesus had, which is told to us in Luke 4:5–8. Here it is written:

> The devil led him up to a high place and showed him in an instant all the kingdoms of the world. And he said to him, "I will give you all their authority and splendor, for it has been given to

me, and I can give it to anyone I want to. So if you worship me, it will all be yours." Jesus answered, "It is written: 'Worship the Lord your God and serve him only.'" (NIV)

Luke doesn't tell us what type of "high place" the devil took Jesus to. However, in order for him to show Jesus "in an instant all the kingdoms of the world" (Luke 4:5 NIV), one can only imagine it must have been a very high place. From this vantage point, Jesus Christ, God's Son saw all that He had created. I wonder how He must have felt when Satan offered Him something that was already His from the beginning of creation. God said in psalm 50, "For every animal of the forest is mine, and the cattle on a thousand hills. I know every bird in the mountains, and the creatures of the field are mine" (Ps. 50:10–11 NIV). The apostle John wrote, "Through him all things were made; without him nothing was made that has been made" (John 1:3 NIV). Jesus knew that everything Satan was showing Him was already His. Satan's promise was an empty promise. Everything was already *His*!

In the same way, we as followers of Christ must come to the same realization that Satan's promises are hollow promises. Satan has nothing to give. Christ already owns all we have. Satan only offers death. Christ offers life. Satan wants us to always look to the past and its failures. Christ owns all of our futures. He alone is the one who gives hope to our promises. Satan seeks to steal and rob of us of what we might have. Jesus alone is the one we turn to for our needs to be met. Satan only wants to bring hurt and despair. Christ alone is the one who brings comfort during our times of trials. Satan wants to condemn us. Jesus Christ, the Son of God, can and wants to forgive us our sins and offer us eternal life. Christ alone is the one who has taught us what the meaning of the word *love* is. It is Him! Jesus Christ, Son of God, our Lord and our Savior! Through Christ alone can our whole world be held in the safety and security of His hands!

Layers

If a person were to drive on Interstate 90, 109 miles east of where Wyoming and South Dakota share a state line, and take Exit 109, they would be faced with having to make a choice between two of the most iconic places that grace the state of South Dakota when they come to the stop sign at the bottom of the exit.

If a person were to turn left there on Highway 240, they would go north into the little town of Wall, South Dakota. Wall may arguably be one of the best-known small towns in our country. Even though they may only host a population of just over 750 people, they are visited by people who drive through this part of the country from most likely every state in America as well as a great number of foreign countries. Signs with the number of miles to Wall Drug have been seen nearly around this world, hailing from places such as Pakistan, Vietnam, Copenhagen, and India. Why people would want to stop to visit Wall Drug on their way through South Dakota is a mystery to many, but the fact that reportedly over one million people a year do is a testimony to the free great-tasting ice water that was the early claim to fame for this small town.

If a person were to turn right at the stop sign at Exit 109, they would head to one of the most unique national parks of this country: Badland's National Park. With the rock and clay formations that line the nearly thirty-mile drive through the park, reaching heights of only a few hundred feet, they don't compare to the five-thousand-foot cliffs of the Grand Canyon. With a landscape that is nearly bare except for the occasional deep-green scrub brush and the occasional Rocky Mountain juniper, the land of the prairies in the park are covered with tall prairie grass that waves briskly in the South Dakota winds at the visitors as they drive by. Whereas the Black Hills of South Dakota, which lie an hour's drive west of the Badlands, sport the tall, dense, deep evergreen-covered hillsides from which they derive their name. The Badlands are known for the rugged beauty of their sand-and-gravel peaks and spires and the abundant wildlife that call this park their home.

There is one other aspect of Badland's National Park that adds immensely to the uniqueness of its character. As a person drives along the main road of the park, the one common feature of the drive is the fact that around each corner, around each curve in the road, the view is as different as can be from the one prior. Most of the park is bathed in the tans and grays of the sand-and-gravel rock formations and towers. However, occasionally, one will come upon areas where the tan and gray layers of the hillsides are divided by the distinct layers of red or orange, which come from the iron oxide material in the hillsides. At another place, there may be layers of shale material that serve as foundational layers to the spires and peaks above and can be recognized by the purple and yellow colors of the soil. Still at another point, layers of white volcanic ash can be evidenced in the makeup of the hillsides. At various times and places, it is possible to see multiple, if not all, of these colors come together to form the layer upon layer of rocky, sandy material that was deposited so many years ago and now make up the beauty of the Badland's National Park. On a clear day, with a beautiful baby-blue South Dakota sky above and the warmth of the early morning sun or the setting evening sun shining over your shoulder, the magnificence of layers upon layers of tan and gray sand separated by the layers of red-and-orange iron oxide and yellow shale and white volcanic ash can be more than enough reason for a person to stand in awe at the beauty and to not be able to utter any other word than "Wow!" Each and every layer of colored material that is seen before you adds in its own unique way to the magnificent stone structures that draw so many people to this park each year.

As I stood before this incredible site one day, I couldn't help but think of how similar the interlocking layers, which my eyes feasted upon this day, were to what we call the Christian experience. For many, when they think of what it means to be a Christian, they might see but a two-dimensional, monochromatic picture. However, for the Christian, God is able to and wants to use each and every layer of the life we possess. Perhaps one layer of our life is representative of the time in our life that was before we became a Christian. Perhaps another layer may be representative of a very different time when we struggled through some very difficult battles in our life. Perhaps another layer might be representative of a time when things went very well and we were able to celebrate great days or victories in life. In the same way that the various deposits of the Badlands all worked together to form the mountains and hills, which we are now blessed with being able to see, our God is able to use the various layers of our life's experiences to make us into the people He needs us to be today. The apostle Paul tells us in 2 Corinthians 11:22–31 about some of the many layers of his Christian experience. Here he writes:

> Are they Hebrews? So am I...Are they Abraham's descendants? So am I...Are they servants of Christ? So am I...Five times I received from the Jews the forty lashes minus one...once I was stoned, three times I was shipwrecked...I have been constantly on the move. I have been in danger from rivers, in danger from bandits, in danger from my own countrymen...I have known hunger and thirst...I have been cold and naked...If I must boast, I will boast of the things that show my weakness. The God and Father of the Lord Jesus, who is to be praised forever, knows that I am not lying... (NIV)

If there was ever anyone who understood the value that all the layers to his life represented, it was the apostle Paul. Paul understood the invaluable testimony that these layers gave of the grace and mercy of his Lord and Savior, Jesus the Christ. Even in the verses such as these where the apostle Paul could have found reason to boast of all he had experienced, he also recognized how in all these things, the layers of his life could be used to bring honor and glory to his Lord and his Savior.

The heart of the apostle Paul can be seen in one of his last, final recorded statements where he states, "But the Lord stood at my side and gave me strength, so that through me the message might be fully proclaimed and all the Gentiles might hear it" (2 Tim. 4:17a NIV). Fellow Christians, can we and may we have the same heart!

Like a Bridge

Our journey this day would take us on a completely different type of path than what so many of our other journeys have been like. Typically, as we traveled from one place to another, our preferred mode of travel was in either our car or truck. Today, the method we chose to use to travel meant picking up one foot and setting it down in front of the other and then repeating this motion many more times until we had fully traversed the path that ran nearly two miles for its round trip.

After driving the approximately eighteen-mile route (which took us from the park entrance to the end of the road), we slowly wove our car among the gathering of the many other vehicles that had been driven over the same route and carefully navigated around the many other people who had the same goal in mind as what we did. Upon finding a parking place in this throng of people, we parked the car, gathered a couple bottles of water for the journey, and set off on our hike.

With a gradual incline to start off with, this hike would seem to be like many of the other hikes we had taken. However, soon the brick-red walls of rock began to rise to nearly fifty feet in the air as they closed in on us from each side, ultimately narrowing our path to only a few feet in width. The pathway would rise and then drop. It would take us to the left and then to the right. At times, there was nothing to be seen except the beautiful red stone walls that outlined our path, juxtaposed against the beautiful high-altitude blue sky. Occasionally, where the walls of the canyon might ease their way back from the pathway some, the occasional juniper tree could be seen with its dark-evergreen colored needles contrasting with the bright-red soil around it. When the pathway opened up even further and the walls stepped back to allow the warmth of the late summer day to reach their surfaces, the lowly desert scrub began to flourish and provide food and cover for the numerous animals and wildlife that called this canyon area of the desert west their home.

For nearly a mile, we would make this journey, only stopping long enough to take a refreshing drink of the warm water from our bottles or to gaze in awe at the incredible beauty of what we recognized as being God's handiwork. Perhaps we might even need to catch our breath after climbing an arduous section of path up a steep incline. Soon, our destination stood in all its majesty before us: the Landscape Arch in Arches National Park.

Rising nearly to the height of the bluffs above it, the Landscape Arch is one of the longest natural stone arches in the world. Connecting the stony hillsides on each end, the Landscape Arch spans over 290 feet. Whereas it might have easily been a hundred feet from the ground below to the top surface of the arch above, the arch itself narrows to as little as six feet in thickness at its crest and perhaps an equal distance in width.

Standing below, gazing up at the majestic structure above, I wondered what it would be like, if it were possible, to be able to make the journey over this arch, from one side to the other. Alone, on the top of the hillside with nowhere else to turn and not being able to go back, what would it be like to make this one-hundred-yard journey to the other side? No other choices. No other options.

This is the choice we need to make as it comes to our relationship with God. We hear about this incredible place we would like to go. We might do research about what or where this place is. We talk with our friends to see what they think of the idea. If there are special people in our lives, we might even decide to have them come along with us as we begin to make the journey. And then we pack our baggage, and we go.

There are times when we might feel like the uphill climb might be too difficult. "I can't do this," we may say to ourselves. "It is too difficult," we cry. *Look at all those who have quit and turned around,* we think. *Is it really worth all this?* But we continue on because there is just something about this bridge that intrigues us and continues to draw us ever onward. Soon we are standing on top of this hill, looking at this very narrow, very tall, and very long bridge before us. The question we all will be confronted with is, "What will we do?"

Scripturally, we are told in John 6:44 that the only way anyone will come to the place where they will make a decision about what they will ultimately do with God will be by God drawing them toward Him. There may be difficulties in our journey toward Him, but He keeps on drawing us ever closer to where we need to be. Sometimes, that feeling of being led along the path may take us into places that are bright and beautiful, and we can only stand in awe as we look at what the hand of God can do and wants to do. There are other times when, as we are compelled along this journey, that the path may become dark and hard. But onward we go. One step at a time. One hill to climb at a time. One bench to rest at, each at the appropriate place we need them to be. And soon, we stand alone at the top of the hill looking at the choice we have to make. Do we continue on, or do we go back? We are confronted with the words that Jesus asked Peter in Matthew 16:15, where He asked Peter, "Who do you say I am?" (NIV).

In 1 Timothy, the apostle Paul wrote, "For there is one God and one mediator between God and men, the man Christ Jesus, who gave himself as a ransom for all men... (1 Tim. 2:5–6 NIV). That long, lonely archway before you is the only way forward, even as Paul tells us that there is only the One mediator between us and a loving God who has drawn us toward Him.

What will we do? We go forward. We must go forward. Our whole journey up to this point is for this particular moment. "But what if I slip and fall?" we ask. We must go on. "Will the stone be strong enough to hold me?" we worry out loud. "What if no one else comes along after me?" we want to know. But we go on, knowing that to turn around and look back to see what the others are doing could result in a fatal fall from this height.

Soon, we realize the archway is still strong. It has held up for many others for as long as anyone can remember. We put our trust in the only One who will bring us to the place we want to be. The narrowest and thinnest portion is now behind us. The other hillside is steadily growing closer. Those on the other side are watching as we take that last, final step safely to the hillside on the other side.

We all must face this question in our own way. What will we do when God confronts us with the question, "Whom do you say my Son, Jesus the Christ, is?" Will we step forward and step out in trust, or will we turn around and go back? That is the question of our lifetime.

The Lord Is My Shepherd

As is the case for most roads that lead from the flatlands and the prairies below, up through the rolling foothills and then on toward the majestic mountains above, Highway 12 in southern Colorado follows no different pattern. Slowly, the open flatland of eastern Colorado begins to take an ever so slight rise as you drive along Highway 350 toward the town of Trinidad, Colorado. Occasionally, you might make the rise and descent of a small hill as you continue along your journey. With the view being unencumbered with the changes in altitude that these hills represent, the views seem endless as they stretch from one horizon to the next. Before long, the rise and fall of the highway begins to be a regular occasion rather than rarity. Much like a giant roller coaster, the blacktop of the road before you rises and falls, twists and turns as you work your way mile after mile westwards toward the great snowcapped mountains, which collectively are called the Rockies. Soon, the hills begin to become steeper, the ridges become more pronounced, the curves tighten, and the valleys seem more pronounced. One thing remains though, the mountains that you are chasing after begin to transform from what look like violet-blue shadows resting lazily on the horizon to the rugged sun-drenched individual peaks that make up the mountain ranges that now carry the names of the Sangre de Christo Mountains, the Wet Mountains, the Spanish Peaks, and the San Juan Mountains of southern Colorado and Northern New Mexico.

As you leave Trinidad and continue on your westward journey up Highway 12, there is one point in particular (though there are many other that are not so noticeable) where you will come around a curve and the view of the valleys below and the mountains above explodes before you. You will see the lush green meadows where the deer and the elk graze. The rolling foothills will rise gently from the grasslands below, up toward the deep-green pine forests that cover the sides of the mighty mountaintop peaks. From this vantage point, you will be able to identify row after row and layer after layer of ever-increasingly taller hilltops and mountains, leading eventually up to the peaks of the beautiful snowcapped mountains in the distance.

In the church, oftentimes we talk about how great the "mountaintop" experiences are in life. When we are on the top of the mountain, we are told of how great things will be and how beautiful the view will be. The exhilaration of having achieved the completion of the climb will be worth whatever struggles occur along the way, or so we are told.

Contrasted to the mountaintop experience are the times when we are "in the valley below." The valley represents to many the difficult times of our life. It is as if the struggles of navigating the winding paths and rocky terrain (which is often associated as being a part of the valley) are somehow supposed to represent the lonely and frightening portions of our journey throughout life.

Perhaps though, as we consider what David wrote in the twenty-third psalm, there is another perspective that we can take as to how we view our spiritual journey. It is here that David wrote:

> The Lord is my shepherd, I shall not be in want. He makes me lie down in green pastures, he leads me beside quiet waters, he restores my soul. He guides me in paths of righteousness for his name's sake. Even though I walk through the valley of the shadow of death, I will fear no evil, for you are with me; your rod and your staff, they comfort me. (Ps. 23:1–4 NIV)

From the perspective of King David (who understood fully what being a shepherd meant), he recognized that the Lord was his shepherd. David knew that even as the shepherd's sheep were in the valley below so also would be the shepherd. Though David knew what it meant to be on top of the very pinnacle of success, he also understood the struggles of life.

As we ponder the meaning of each of these phrases, we can begin to better understand the picture that David wanted to paint for us of the One he loved. David recognized that his God, and the God of his fathers, would be the answer to all his needs. While there were times in which God would provide for his needs to be met, there were also times when God would only lead him to where he could take care of his needs himself.

A good shepherd knew where the green pastures and the quiet waters could be found. Green pastures are the source of plentiful food. Still waters are representative of waters that run deep. Bountiful food and the abundance of fresh, clear life-giving water meant a state of rest and restoration of strength could be found.

David trusted in his Lord for the direction and guidance he would need in his life. Even though the sheep might find food and water and rest where they were, there was always a need for fresh resources of food and drink. David trusted in the faithfulness of his God to provide him with that guidance.

David also understood there most likely would be some dark and dangerous times in the life of the shepherd and his flock. But he knew these times were only a shadow of what they could be or might have been intended to be. David knew he didn't need to fear these difficult times because his Shepherd would be there with him, protecting him, leading him, and providing for his needs. David understood firsthand that a good shepherd is one who is always there for those whom are entrusted to his care.

Gracious Heavenly Father, we recognize that you alone are the one in whom we can put our trust. Father, would you help us to learn to accept the guidance you give through the presence of your Holy Spirit? Would you give us the courage to walk with you, even when the path around us seems to be filled with traps and snares? Gracious God, we honor you and give you the praise for all the blessings and provisions that you alone have provided. Help us to trust you and to seek the joys of our relationship with you each day. In Jesus's name, Amen.

White as Snow

Whether you have only lived and traveled in one area of our great country, or whether you have traveled extensively around its nearly four million square miles, or whether you have lived in many of the regions and states of this great land, there is one thing which most people will agree on: the beauty of God's creation can be evidenced at every turn and every corner of this place we call home.

For those who call the Gulf Coast of the state of Florida home, there is no greater beauty than sitting on the warm, white sandy shores of the beach, watching the brilliant orange glow of the evening sun setting on the Gulf of Mexico as the waves gently slap upon the shoreline that lays at their feet. For those people who live in a place called Chicago, the ice formations, which are created on the rocks and railings of the city shoreline, formed as the windswept waves come in off Lake Michigan, may find their hearts as impressed as if they were viewing the works of the best of sculptors. As one stands on the shores of the mighty, thundering Niagara River and watches... and listens...and feels the body-shaking power of the water as it falls and tumbles over the mighty Niagara Falls, they are reminded of how powerless and insignificant man can be at times. The person who stands in awe on the edge of the beautiful brick-red walls of the Grand Canyon of northwestern Arizona while gazing down over five thousand feet to the raging waters of the Colorado River may find the view literally breathtaking. For the person who finds themselves in the mountains of the eastern United States in the cool, crisp days of early fall, it may be difficult to fully comprehend the immense beauty seen as the leaves begin to make their change from the summer greens to the reds, yellows, and oranges of the autumn season.

However, there is one other aspect of the natural beauty that can be witnessed in our great land but which is overlooked by many.

As I looked out the window today at the freshly falling snow that was lazily drifting down from the heavens above, I couldn't help but think about other journeys I have made driving through the Big Horn Mountains to our west, the Sangre de Christo Mountains to our south, the Black Hills in our area, and even the Appalachian Mountains to our east. I can think of few things more beautiful than driving up and down the highways of these areas. The pine and fir trees stand tall with their branches reaching for the sky above. The deer and the elk lazily graze in the fields to the left and right. The waters of the streams bubble up and over the rocks and tumble down the water falls on either side of the road. The mountain and hilltops cast their ever-increasing shadows over the trees and roads ahead, even though the sun is far from setting for the night. And then…the snow begins to fall.

At first, the snowflakes are only the tiniest of specks of frozen water, wafting down from the sky above. However, as the temperatures continue to fall one degree at a time and the snows continue, the flakes get bigger and more numerous. The winds begin to blow the accumulating snow; and the barren grounds, which were once hidden by the abundance of the overhead branches above, begin to become covered with the drifting snow. The sturdy evergreen branches, which hold up to the mightiest of summer storms and winds, now begin to gently bow their tips toward the ground below. The rocks that line the shores of the mountain streams become harder and harder to see among the ever-growing covering of snow. The farmhouses and barns still bear witness of where they stand due to the barn-red paint that covers their sides. Even the cattle and the livestock in the fields around begin to find the snow accumulating on their backs as they stand with the wind behind them. It is as if by this tiniest, most singular of all acts of creation, the tiny snowflakes have become one giant unified blanket that covered everything upon which it fell.

As we look at the snow in this way, we are drawn to a verse in the Bible, where the prophet Isaiah wrote, "'Come now, let us reason together,' says the Lord, 'Though your sins are like scarlet, they shall be as white as snow; though they are red as crimson, they shall be like wool'" (Isa. 1:18 NIV). Isaiah, as he was calling the northern nation of Israel to repent and turn back to the God of their fathers, was not doing something new by reminding them that God was desiring them to be a holy people. He was only reminding them that from the very beginning of time, God was inviting His people to come home to Him and be the people they were created to be: a holy people wholly devoted to their relationship with their Creator and their God.

In this prophetic verse, we can see how even as the snow, which falls softly and gently from the sky above covers everything below it, so also does His saving work (which Jesus Christ did by being crucified, dying, and rising again from the grave) cover all the sins of our lives. Even as the fresh snowfall of winter covers everything from the rocks on the ground to the tips of the mountains and the hillsides above, the saving work that Jesus the Christ performed for us covers all our sins, from what we might think are the least even up to the greatest. The apostle Paul wrote in his second letter to the Corinthians, "My grace is sufficient for you..." (2 Cor. 12:9 NIV). The love that was demonstrated for us by the death and resurrection of God's only son on the cross is sufficient price for all those things that we have done that might come between us and our Heavenly Father. In the same way that neither the mighty pine tree nor the mountain is too big to be covered by the falling snow, neither are the sins of our life too big to be covered by God's love and grace. The only difference between the two is that where we have no choice but to accept the beautiful covering of white on the ground before us, because of His love, God allows or gives us the option of accepting the gift of His grace.

Have you accepted His grace and love yet today? Have you allowed Him to turn those deep-red crimson stains of your life into the beauty of the freshly fallen snow? If not, will you today?

Gracious Father, I don't understand all there is to know about you, but I do believe you love me, and that Jesus, your Son, died on the cross for me to pay the price for my sins. Dear God, I am sorry for those things I have done that have made your heart sad. Will you forgive me? I accept the gift of your love and want to live in relationship with you, even like a child does with his father. Thank you God for all you have done and want to do. In Jesus's name, Amen and Amen.

The Light of the World

As I looked out my back door, I was treated to one of the true beauties of winter: watching the freshly falling snow softly drifting down from the layer of moisture-laden clouds that seemed to hang just above the treetops. The tiniest of snowflakes seemed to drop nearly perpendicular to the earth with nary a hint of wind to move them along from side to side. The footprints whose edges were crisp and sharp this morning now had edges and shapes that were softened and hidden by this new covering of white. As I stood there in the door, I couldn't help but be overcome with the volume of the silence that I was now a part of.

However, there is one other aspect that must be experienced in order that one may fully appreciate the totality of the beauty. The streetlight, which is woefully inadequate to illuminate this same backyard during the darkness of the summer months, now brings a warm, soft glow to everything that is in the reaches of its beams of light on this cold snow-covered evening. As the light from the streetlamp reflects off the winter snow, one might easily be able to make their way about the yard or the driveway or the streets of this mountainside town. The footprints that I had left behind, the tracks of the neighborhood cat leading over to go under the shed in the yard, the strings of colored lights that hang from the neighbor's buildings, and the outlines of the mountainside that are just blocks from our backyard are all easily seen from the vantage point of my back door as I stand and look out in this all-encompassing silence of this evening's snow. As well, if one looks ever so closely at the mountaintops to the right, the red star of Christmas can be seen as it spreads its light over the city.

As I considered the absolute beauty of all that I took in, I had to consider what this all means, as it regards being a Christian in our world today. Jesus tells us in John 8:12, where He was speaking of Himself, "I am the light of the world. Whoever follows me will never walk in darkness, but will have the light of life" (NIV). However, He also tells us in Matthew 5:14–16:

> You are the light of the world. A City on a hill cannot be hidden. Neither do people light a lamp and put it under a bowl. Instead they put it on its stand, and it gives light to everyone in the house. In the same way, let your light shine before men… (NIV)

Tonight, as I looked out into this winter night's scene, I was reminded of how we need to be a light in the dark corners of our world. If it weren't for the light reflecting nature of this newly fallen snow, much of the beauty of what existed around me would be lost in the darkness of the night. As Christians, are we diligently working to be reflective of the light that has shown down on us, to all that fall within the realm or sphere of our world? Are we being a light to the world of darkness in which we are placed?

I also was made aware again of how there is nothing that will ever replace the truth represented in the beauty and the ruggedness of the star on the hillside above. Throughout this evening's snowstorm, that star stood there casting its beacon of light and hope over everything that we were blessed with being able to see. Is it perhaps that the "light of the world" (which speaks of Jesus the Christ) is best able to shine His light in the darkness where we live when we as "the light of the world" allow ourselves to be used as instruments of reflection? Is it in this way that the world can see the immense beauty of all that He has created, both in the creation around us as well as in the heart of man? When darkness and light meet, it is the light that will always overcome the darkness of the world that surrounds it.

More than Conquerors

It was a brisk fall morning as the car headed north on the interstate toward an appointment in nearby Pueblo. The early morning sun was rising behind and to the right, which made the western skies over the mountains an even bolder azure blue than usual. It was against this brilliant blue that the Spanish Peaks Mountains rose in the sky off to the left, in an attempt to reach out to touch the nearly full moon, which was still evident in the western sky. The freshly fallen snow, which had accumulated on the top of the Peaks, coursed down the side of the rocky crags and peaks of the mountaintops to where it met up with the greenish black of the evergreens, which rose up from the valley floors, as if the two areas were in some great battle to project their control over the sides of the mountains. Whereas the attention of my focus had been, to this point, zoomed in to consider the mountaintops and the surrounding skies, it was now as if my sight panned back out, like the zoom lens of a camera, to take in the beautiful colors of the surrounding trees in the valleys below. The lime-green leaves of the trees not yet fully changed, the goldenrod colored leaves of the aspens, the crimson reds of the maples, and the caramel-colored tans of the leaves that had passed the prime of their seasonal changes all created a palette that the most talented artist would envy. It was upon this foreground of the beauty of the valleys that the backdrop of the mountain peaks rose from. It also was after the witnessing of the entirety of the beauty of this scene when the understanding came.

In our Christian experience, we oftentimes find we battle between the joys and pure work that God has done in our lives and the dark, difficult times of our struggles. The fatigue and weariness of the battle that we call life wages war with the indescribable beauty of the work that only God has been able to do. When we look closely at, and focus on this battle, we lose sight of the true situation that we find ourselves in. Instead of remembering the healing that has taken place, we see only scars. Instead of having an attitude of gratefulness, we harbor resentment. Instead of standing in awe at all God has done and accomplished for and through us, we want to lick our wounds and wrap ourselves up in a state of self-pity. It is only when we can step back in our vision that we can see the incredible beauty of all that God has done to bring us to where we are. Perhaps we can give consideration to the thought that it is *not* in spite of our difficulties and trials that we have become who we are, but it *is* rather because of our struggles that God has been able to mold us into the vessels for which He has designed us.

In the book of Romans, Paul wrote, "I consider that our present sufferings are not worth comparing with the glory that will be revealed in us" (Rom. 8:18 NIV). Later in the same chapter, he went on to write:

> And we know that in all things God works for the good of those who love him, who have been called according to his purpose...What, then, shall we say in response to this? If God is for us, who can be against us?... Who shall separate us from the love of Christ? Shall trouble or hardship or persecution or famine or nakedness or danger or sword?... No in all these things we are more than conquerors through him who loved us. For I am convinced that neither death nor life, neither angels nor demons, neither the present nor the future, nor any powers, neither height nor depth, nor anything else in all creation, will be able to separate us from the love of God that is in Christ Jesus our Lord. (Romans 8:28, 31, 35–39 NIV)

For the athlete who practices and runs drills time after time, the muscles are stretched and developed to the point where they provide the needed strength and endurance for game day. For the child who is learning to ride the bicycle for the first time, how many bumps, bruises, and spills typically happen before the first victorious ride occurs? For the person learning to play the instrument, how many hours and hours of practice developing sore lips and tired fingers must first be endured before the beautiful music at the final concert can be heard? For the soldier in the field fighting for their very life and breath, how many times did they want to give up during prior training, when they just knew they couldn't go on any further but are now finding victory on the field of battle before them? For the newborn baby struggling to begin their new life outside the womb, how important is it to take that first, deep breath as they try to begin the next phase of their life? Whether it is during those struggles that we go through during the physical times of our lives or whether it is during the battles we face in our spiritual life, a rule of life is that struggle precedes strength.

Even though Jesus, who would ultimately die on the cross for you and for me, may have prayed, "Father, take this cup from me" (Mark 14:36a NIV), he didn't stop there, but went on to finish that prayer by saying, "Yet not what I will, but what you will" (Mark 14:36b NIV). In spite of being fully aware of the struggles and great difficulties that lay ahead for Him, our Lord and Savior endured the shame and punishment of going to the cross for us so that we might be able to live in relationship with Him. The question then becomes, are we willing to do the same for Him?

JACK DROSTE

Contrasts

After spending the night in the little town of Beatty, Nevada, we set out on the next leg of our journey. For the first day of fall, our weather was everything we could ask for. The sky was a deep coral blue with the sporadic clouds being blown along as if they were giant hot-air balloons out for an afternoon flight. The high temperatures for our destination today were expected to be in the upper eighties. Though this may seem high, it was only a week ago our destination was still having temperatures in the triple digits and was expecting to have triple-digit temperatures again the following week. The wind was blowing softly down the valley through which we would go, channeled by the hillsides that rose up on either side.

After we had driven up and over the hills and rises that surround the town of Beatty, we looked westward to the valley below. We watched as Nevada Highway 374 ran as straight and true as an arrow for the next twelve miles. It descended from the hillside around Beatty, ran across the bottom of the desert valley below, and then rose again as it began the uphill climb over the Grapevine Mountains and Funeral Mountains to the west. These two mountain ranges provide the eastern boundary for one of the most desolate places in our country, a place called Death Valley.

Death Valley is a place like no other place I have ever experienced. The floor of the valley itself, which bears the name Death Valley, is long and flat and runs between two mountain ranges that parallel the valley floor on each side. The sides of the mountains on either side of the valley floor are course and rough. These are not the picturesque, tranquil mountains that one normally enjoys seeing in pictures or movies. They are course and violent in appearance, certainly adding to the legitimacy of the name of this place.

To the south and west of the valley floor rise several mountain peaks that stretch upwards in the sky from 12,000 feet to over 14,000 feet. In comparison, one will find much of the flatlands of the valley below to be below sea level, with one area in particular, being some 282 feet below sea level.

The desert floor is largely plain and barren in appearance, broken up by the occasional section of desert scrub trying to live in a desert land of stone and rock. The only coloration of the desert floor, other than the bright white salt flats, the mustard-yellow dunes that appear only in rare areas, and the light browns and tans of the desert shrubs are the small bright lime-green bushes that occasionally dot the landscape. In contrast, the mountain walls, while being very rough, course, and angry in texture, provided some of the most beautiful blends of colors one can imagine. In one place, one might see the mustard-yellow dunes with their tops covered with a dark-chocolate brown layer. Here, it is as if one was looking at the largest bowl of French vanilla ice cream imaginable, covered with an overflowing topping of chocolate syrup. There is another section, which is aptly called the Artist's Palette. In this one small valley, there is an unparalleled collection of the most beautiful of reds, whites, greens, purples, and all the variations of tans and browns one could dream of. Many of these colors are representative of the different types of minerals and soils that have collected in this one spot. In other areas of the park, the deep brick-red soil and stones, which derive their color from the oxidation of the iron that makes up their content, are joined together with perfect layers of white, as if somehow forming a giant layered cake.

As I gave consideration to this study of contrasts, I was drawn to another picture of contrasts that is told to us in the Bible. This story is the story of a beggar named Lazarus and a rich man. In this life, the beggar had little to cover himself except the sores on his body, while the rich man was dressed in the finest clothes possible. The beggar hoped he might be lucky enough to be able to eat the crumbs that fell from the rich man's table, while the rich man had all he needed. In this life, the only commonality between the two men was that they both died.

Regarding their deaths, it says:

> The time came when the beggar died and the angels carried him to Abraham's side. The rich man also died and was buried. In hell, where he was in torment, he looked up and saw Abraham far away, with Lazarus by his side. So he called to him, "Father Abraham, have pity on me and send Lazarus to dip the tip of his finger in water and cool my tongue, because I am in agony in this fire." (Luke 16:22–24 NIV)

As we traveled about Death Valley this day, the contrasts that we witnessed were stark. Where one was flat and even below sea level, the other reached for nearly three miles up into the air. Where one showed only the slightest of colors and was unassuming, the other was angry and menacing yet bountiful in color. While the beautiful white snow that might be seen later in the year on the mountain peaks above would represent a fresh and cool air, the valley below was home to some of the hottest temperatures ever recorded in our country.

In the story above from the book of Luke, I believe we also can see stark differences between where the rich man was going to face his eternity and the place where Lazarus would spend his.

It is notable that we only know the name of the man, Lazarus, and not of the one called the rich man. How incredible is it that our God knows our name!

What comfort it is to also note that for Lazarus, it says he was taken up to be at the side of Abraham. For the rich man, it only says that he died and he was buried. Can we find comfort in knowing that even in death, God hasn't forgotten us?

The picture that is painted of heaven is one of Lazarus being next to his ancestor, Father Abraham. Though not stated, the picture painted is one of family, of security, of provisions, and of rest. For the rich man, he speaks of torment, agony, fear, and fire.

What hope we are able to have knowing that we serve a God who knows us and will call us by name. He will continue to provide for us throughout all eternity. We will be safe and secure, and we will be able to rest in the place He has made for us.

However, for those who don't know the one we call Lord and Savior, the eternity ahead looks to be one of loneliness and isolation, of fear and of agony. The difference between the two is as real as the difference between life and death.

Gracious Father, as we consider the differences between these two eternal destinations, would You help us also consider the fact that the choice is ours and ours alone. The one is with an ever-loving God who knows us by name, cares for us, and comforts us. The other place where we might choose to spend our eternity is a place of despair, agony, and fear. Father, strengthen us, encourage us, forgive us and teach us to walk in your ways. Let our hearts be turned toward You. In the name of Jesus, the Christ, your Son. Amen and Amen.

A Living Memorial

As is the case for many of the places that exist around our great country, the Black Hills of South Dakota richly abound in the heritage and life of the many days gone by. One of the many towns that is found within the confines of the northern Black Hills can be found about a half hour down Highway 85, nestled in and among the pine tree forests and near the one-thousand-foot-tall yellow limestone cliffs of the nearby canyons. This town is called Deadwood, South Dakota.

When one approaches the main street of Deadwood, South Dakota, one is immediately reminded of the scene that others might have seen nearly 150 years ago. Gone are the wood-plank sidewalks, which would have been laid out like ribbons, in front of the many storefronts that lined the main street. The dirt-and-mud street has now been replaced with rows of immaculately placed bricks. Gone are the tents that might have held residence along the main street as are the stores and businesses of the many Chinese immigrants that inhabited this area. Where horses and buggies once were driven down the streets and along the hills, rows of modern cars and trucks now make their journeys. The place that lays claim to being the original location of Saloon # 10 (where Wild Bill Hickok was shot) can be found, even though the original building burned down in a fire over 130 years ago. However, across the street and down the block, the new location where the original business moved to and rebuilt can also still be found.

As one heads south from the downtown area, the drive can be made up the steeply inclined narrow street that leads to a place called Mount Moriah. Mount Moriah is the primary cemetery that services Deadwood and is located high above the town on the very steep sides of the hill that overlooks the town below. It is in this cemetery where one can find the final resting spots of many of the early inhabitants of the town, including two of its most famous: Wild Bill Hickok and Calamity Jane.

While we walked the streets and paths of this town on this early fall day, I was reminded of so many of the historical facts that serve as the foundation for the heritage of this little town nestled among the Black Hills of South Dakota. I wondered what it would have been like to walk these streets and have a character such as Wild Bill approach me on boardwalks of the street. What would it have been like to have been able to witness a giant dragon parading down the street as the community celebrated the Chinese New Year? Can one imagine what it would have felt like to have watched as Crooked Nose Jack McCall ran from Saloon #10 after infamously firing that fatal shot that killed the famous Mr. Hickok? Undoubtedly, many of the modern-day visitors to this quaint, picturesque town high up in the Black Hills of South Dakota would be able to recite many of these same facts. Undoubtedly, it is because of these same facts that many are drawn to even consider visiting this magnet of history

Standing there under the umbrella of the evergreen pines that cover the hills of Mount Moriah, I was reminded of another time when someone was called to build a structure that would serve as a reminder to all who followed of what had happened at that spot. In the fourth chapter of the book of Joshua, God (through the man Joshua) is leading His people, the nation of Israel, along the final path of their journey. This journey had taken them from the lifestyle of captivity that they had experienced while living in Egypt to the flood swollen shores of the Jordan River and the lands that God had promised to them as their new home. In Joshua 4:2, God spoke these words to Joshua:

> Choose twelve men from among the people, one
> from each tribe, and tell them to take up twelve
> stones from the middle of the Jordan from right
> where the priests stood and to carry them over

with you and put them down at the place where
you stay tonight. (NIV)

Joshua gave additional information about the purpose of what
God had told him to do a few verses later when he said in verses 5–7
of Joshua 4:

> Each of you is to take up a stone on his shoulder…
> to serve as a sign among you. In the future, when
> your children ask you, "What do these stones
> mean?" tell them that the flow of the Jordan
> was cut off before the ark of the covenant of the
> LORD. When it crossed the Jordan, the waters of
> the Jordan were cut off. These stones are to be a
> memorial to the people of Israel forever. (NIV)

In the construction of this altar of stones, gathered from the
middle of the once raging waters of the Jordan River, God called His
people to build a memorial that would serve as a reminder to all generations to come of what it was that God had done as only He could
do. God used man's hands as the instruments to build this memorial.
In the years to come, future generations would learn that it was God's
hands that were able to stop the flood waters of the Jordan in order
that the nation of Israel could cross over it on dry land. These same
generations of the years to come would also be able to learn of God's
faithfulness in bringing to completion the promise of His word and
how He provided for and protected His people through the many
years of wandering throughout the desert lands.

The same questions still beg to be asked even today in our
personal relationships with our Lord and our God. Have we built
memorials to those things we have done, or have we based and built
our memorials on those things that God has done, perhaps through
the use of our hands? When we look back to the memories of our
lives and ministries, do we recognize and honor those things that we
know only the hand of God could have accomplished? As we look
also at those times of our lives when we might not understand how

certain things could have happened, are we willing to acknowledge that we are only able to look out at the memorable events of our lives because of the faithfulness and goodness of the one we call lord?

May our goal always be to bring honor and glory to the *one* to whom it belongs!

Who We Are

For those of us who love living in smaller communities, we do so because we see several benefits that we receive by staying further away from the masses that make up the bigger cities. Normally, we perceive we have a greater sense of physical security. All too often, the horrific crimes we hear about are usually reported as happening in the bigger cities of our states. We also seem to feel more of a hometown feeling in a smaller community than what we do in a larger city. Driving down the streets of our towns, we like to wave to those we know in other vehicles; or those who might be walking down the sidewalk; or are even those who might be sitting on their porches, sipping on a cup of coffee or a glass of tea, watching the traffic go by.

There are, however, advantages to living in the larger communities. The best possibilities for good employment are found in larger cities. In the larger cities, the greatest variety of places to eat and shop are found. To the city, one usually has to go in order to find the best opportunities for medical care for all our needs. So it was for reasons such as these that on this day we bundled up in the car and started to head north on I-25 toward Pueblo.

For most of the nearly one-hundred-mile trip north, we drove past mile after mile of dry desert lands to our right where hardly a building is be seen and where only the greenery of the desert scrub and prairie grasses break up the monotony of the barren sandy tan-colored grounds. To our left, the mountain ranges to the west begin to rise like a frontline defense against the encroachment of the prairie lands. We drove past one rocky hillside that resembles a giant crocodile with its spiny back resting on the prairie floors, basking in the heat of the sun. A little further along stands the remains of an ancient volcano, reminding one of how so much of this landscape was created. For the first sixty miles of our trip, though the scenery seemed to always be changing, it also seemed to always remain the same.

Before long, we began our uphill approach to the exit that we needed to take for the combined cities of Rye and Colorado City. We turned west toward Colorado City and, after driving through this little community, began to make our way up into the mountains on Highway 165. Soon, we began to make our way around one curve then the next. As we left the dry, barren prairies below, we started to make our climb in altitude as we drove around one curve to the next. Here, on our right, was a lush green meadow where one might envision seeing the herds of deer coming down to feed in the evening. Then, a little later, we could see on the mountain side of the road where they had to cut away a part of the hillside in order for the road to go through. We soon found ourselves in the midst of the thick dark-evergreen forests that lined our path on either side. Where there was no snow further down on the desert plains, we now began to see the occasional pile of snow, as if hiding under the protection of the pine branches. On the left, we passed one of the many mountain lakes of this area: to the right, a quiet meandering stream working its way down the valley side. In every way, with the blue skies above and all the beauty of God's creation around us, this was shaping up to be a typical relaxing day driving through the mountains of Colorado. Before long though, we came to our first stop on this portion of our journey to Pueblo.

Here, sitting on a two-to three-acre plot of land at nine thousand feet in elevation is an unbelievable man-made edifice that is well known as Bishop's Castle to locals and visitors alike. Bishop's Castle is the creation of a single individual by the name of Jim Bishop. This limestone-and-iron castle rises nearly five stories in the air and would be the dream of every medieval warlord. Every stone, every step, every piece of ornamental iron that is now a part of this castle has been put into place by Mr. Bishop. From the three-story stone staircase ascending up the front of the castle to the stone turrets that you can climb by way of internal iron stairwells to the top of the cathedral-style ceiling that covers the main gathering area and even on to the hand-crafted stainless steel fire-breathing dragon's head, Mr. Bishop has built a magnificent castle that would rival anything the finest science fiction movie could offer. Stone by stone, step by step, one piece of iron and steel after another, Jim Bishop has crafted by himself something no one else has ever done.

Standing in awe at what this man has done over the last several decades by himself, I couldn't help but wonder what it must be like to have not only the creative talents he has to design such a thing, but to also have the mechanical and architectural abilities to take what his mind can envision and actually build it with his hands. How many of us would love to be Mr. Bishop and do what he has done?

But then, I was reminded of what the apostle Paul wrote in the book of Ephesians. In Ephesians 4:11–13, Paul wrote these words speaking of Jesus:

> He who gave some to be apostles, some to be prophets, some to be evangelists, and some to be pastors and teachers, to prepare God's people for works of service, so that the body of Christ may be built up until we all reach unity in the faith and in the knowledge of the Son of God and become mature, attaining to the whole measure of the fullness of Christ. (NIV)

Too many times we get caught up in wishing we could do those things that someone is able to do. We watch the athletes on television and wish we could do what they do so we could be paid what they are paid. Or perhaps, we wish we could paint like the famous artist did, whose picture we are now admiring in a world-class museum. Maybe our wish is to be able to be good at public speaking or singing so we can wow the audiences before us with the melodious sounds of our voice. Or perhaps, we might find one of any number of any other ways we could live the life of and have the talents that another has.

In these verses from Ephesians, the compassion of our Father shines through as He reassures us in His Word, that *He* is the one who calls and appoints all of us to the various positions that we fill in life. How comforting it is for the one who God called to be a pastor to know that it was God indeed that called them to that task. However, it also would be comforting to the one called to the task that may not be so noticeable that they also are as called to their task as is the one who stands or performs before the larger crowds.

In 1 Corinthians 12:12, the apostle Paul also wrote these words: "The body is a unit, though it is made up of many parts; and though all its parts are many, they form one body. So it is with Christ" (NIV). Let us be encouraged by knowing that in whatever position we may find in life and with whatever talents we might be given, they are given by and are appointed by God. Our worth in God's eyes does not increase nor does it decrease by the level or rank in life we hold. The example that Jesus left us shows us that the greatest leader in life needs to be willing to be the greatest servant. As well, the one who joyfully and obediently fulfills their role as the lowest servant in life will become one of the greatest leaders we may meet. Let's not forget Paul's charge in Colossians 3:17, "And whatever you do, whether in word or deed, do it all in the name of the Lord Jesus, giving thanks to God the Father through him" (NIV). Let us do whatever we do because we know God has anointed and called us for that task in life. Let's do so with all our heart as unto the Lord. Let's give thanks for who we are.

A Better Way

For most of my working life, my jobs of choice have often involved driving over the road in some manner. At times, it was a job that required delivering packages to homes and businesses throughout the communities that were surrounded by the never-ending corn and soybean fields of eastern and southern Minnesota and Iowa. At other times, it was driving a delivery vehicle and service van throughout the woodlands and cities of the western Gulf Coast of Florida, where I was responsible for the installation and maintenance of soft drink beverage equipment. Even though the view from the office windows would seemingly remain the same forever, the view from my van might change at any given mile. At one turn, I might be watching the waves of the Gulf of Mexico slapping against the sandy shores. A few miles later, my eyes would feast on the view of a cypress swamp, where the ever-elusive alligator would be watching silently for its next meal. Later on, perhaps even on the same day, I might find myself driving for miles through a tree-formed archway, where, because of the interwoven branches and leaves overhead, I was presented with the opportunity to drive through one of the most beautiful of tunnels one could imagine. In each place we lived, whether it was in the farmlands of Iowa; or in the tropical beauty of Florida, or even when it ended up being in the desert climates of South Dakota, New Mexico, and Colorado, and regardless of the weather, my hunger to see the concrete of the highway rolling out behind me like a long gray ribbon was never fully satisfied.

However, even as it is with anyone who has ever driven up and down the mountains, or across the desert, or through the winding roads that snake throughout a forest, one common experience that most of us have had is coming to the point when we aren't sure where we are and how to get to where we want to go. Sometimes it might be because we received wrong or poor directions from a person who believed they were in the know. Sometimes it might be due to a lack of familiarity with the local culture or history of the community. The checker at the local gas station, who has lived in their community for all of their life, may very well remember where that old tree used to be in the middle of that intersection out on some back country gravel road on the way to Farmer Joe's place. However, for a new person, wanting to make their first delivery to Farmer Joe's home, a tree that used to be there, but which was blown over or cut down perhaps thirty years ago is of little help in being able to be used as a means to follow the directions given. Still, there might even be other reasons why we might get lost, such as because of inaccurate maps and Global Positioning Systems, which are better recognized by the initials GPS. Maps become outdated and inaccurate, if they were even correct in the first place. In regards to GPS, I have heard stories of and have seen how a person has ended up blocks away from their destination, or even out in the middle of some deserted field or desert, as they waited for directions from the nice young lady who sits on the dashboard of their vehicle and constantly reminded them of their need to "recalculate" or to turn here or there where no road exists.

As I thought of these two issues of how and why we end up getting lost, my thoughts turned to those words that are written in the books of Psalms and Proverbs and what it means to us in our Christian walk.

In Psalm 1:1, we read, "Blessed is the man who does not walk in the counsel of the wicked or stand in the way of sinners..." (Ps. 1:1 NIV). We can compare what we read there in Psalm 1 to what King Solomon wrote in Proverbs 3:5–6, where he says, "Trust in the Lord with all your heart and lean not on your own understanding; in all your ways acknowledge him, and he will make your paths straight" (NIV). As we consider what these two writers wrote respectively, we see where, on the one hand, the psalmist cautions us against putting our trust and confidence in the directions that are given to us by those whom the author calls "wicked" or "sinners." On the other hand, King Solomon tells us though, that it is good and proper to put our trust in the One whom the Jewish people recognized as being the One who created them and gave them the very breath of life. Who we turn to as we seek advice regarding the direction of where we are heading in life can make all the difference in the world. Has the one we are seeking directions from already gone in the same direction as what we are wanting to go? Do they know firsthand of the journey that we are on? Are they offering advice and guidance while looking on from outside the realm of personal experience? The words that Solomon wrote in Proverbs are offered up from the perspective of one who realized and acknowledged that the one he called Lord was far greater than what he, Solomon, was. Solomon's wisdom taught him that as we seek out advice and direction, we don't want to go to those who might have no understanding of the journey we are on but rather we go to one such as our Lord and God, who was the one that created us in the beginning.

The second issue I considered, as it pertained to being lost, is the reliability of the message itself. Not only do we have to look at the nature of the one giving the directions, but we also have to give consideration to the reliability of the plans or directions themselves. Even a person who has never been on a particular journey before can navigate the trip safely if the directions are proper. However, it is much more comforting for the traveler who is lost to be able to hear from the one who is giving directions, "I know it is true. I've been there before."

The author of Hebrews wrote, "Because he himself suffered when he was tempted, he is able to help those who are being tempted" (Heb. 2:18 NIV). He also wrote, "For we do not have a high priest who is unable to sympathize with our weaknesses, but we have one who has been tempted in every way, just as we are—yet was without sin" (Heb. 4:15 NIV). Jesus lived as we do here on earth and was tempted, but He lived a life above the temptations set before Him. He can direct our pathways to do the same.

Jesus said, "I am the way and the truth and the life. No one comes to the Father except through me" (John 14:6 NIV). Jesus has seen the Father and has been in His presence. Jesus knows what it takes for us to see the Father someday for ourselves.

Jesus also said, "In my Father's house are many rooms…" (John 14:2 NIV). He has been there. His word is trustworthy.

From Hebrews again, we read, "Therefore, since we have a great high priest who has gone through the heavens, Jesus the Son of God, let us hold firmly to the faith we profess" (Heb. 4:14 NIV).

What a joy and a privilege it is to know that the One who promises to give directions and purpose to the pathways of our lives is One who has walked the paths we have to walk in life, all the while remaining faithful and true in His relationship with our Father. In Him, not only can we put our trust, but we must. Let us put our trust in the only One who can truly say, "I know it is true. I've been there before!"

But Why God Why

Therefore the Lord himself will give you a sign:
the virgin will conceive and give birth to a son,
and will call him Immanuel. (Isa. 7:14 NIV)

For to us a child is born, to us a son is given, and
the government will be on his shoulders. And he
will be called Wonderful Counselor, Mighty God,
Everlasting Father, Prince of Peace. (Isa. 9:6 NIV)

On this cool winter day, in a city far from where we call home, we find ourselves sitting in a hospital this morning, waiting on the hands of the doctors, surgeons, and staff to finish with the unexpected task that was presented before them this day. Instead of driving about looking at the beautiful lights that typically decorate homes of friends and neighbors during this joyous season, we are staring at IVs, and hospital parking garages, and surgical gowns and waiting rooms. With no Christmas tree put up at home, nor a single Christmas card mailed out, not a present bought, or a promise of our typical Christmas feast being prepared, my thoughts began to wonder about what the true meaning of Christmas really is.

As I thought about this normally joyous season where we celebrate the birth of our Savior in a cold, dark, damp manger near the town of Bethlehem of Judea, I began to wonder why it was that the God of all heaven and earth would choose to begin His earthly ministry in the form of a baby. Why not come as a king leading an eternal army? Why not come as an all-knowing wise man on a mountaintop? Why did He come as a helpless yet adorable baby to be coddled and nursed and embraced in the arms of a young mother and her husband?

One lesson I can learn from this action by our God is that there may be no better example of, nor more universally accepted symbol of pure love, than to witness the love and the joy expressed through the smile of a newborn baby. For those women whom I have known (who have given birth to a baby), there is no medicine that can be given that is more powerful than what it is to hold their newborn child in their arms for the first time. As the first sounds of their child's cry reaches their ears and their newly born child snuggles up close against their cheek and chest, their experience of pure, unmitigated joy and love is something that is remembered throughout their lifetime. Though the photos that are taken show the strains of the sweat that has coursed down their brow or hairstyles that would never be considered for public viewing under any other circumstances, the joy of the love, which can be seen in the eyes of the mother and child, is unmistakable. Perhaps our Father knew that the best lesson of love is that which is demonstrated through the eyes and smile and touch of a baby.

There is a second lesson that I believe we can take from this fact of history. By being born as a baby, perhaps we, who seek to walk in relationship with our God, are better able to understand the responsibility that we bear in sharing and nurturing this message of love that has been so beautifully given. The shy young mother is eager to show off the gift of love that she has been given to all the world around her. The usually fearful young father is often the primary bearer of good news to the friends and family around as he calls them to come and look at his newborn son or daughter. The extended family will often come together to help the young couple rejoice over their newfound joy. Presents are given. Assistance is offered. Needs are met. Even though the greatest expression of love that can be given has been given in the form of this baby, the responsibility for the sharing and spreading of this message of love to others has been accepted by and performed by those to whom this bundle has been entrusted.

There is a third lesson that I believe we can glean from this biblical account of the birth of Jesus, which we celebrate each year at this time. The baby Jesus was born in a borrowed stable to a young couple who may have been (at least in our society's thinking) middle class to lower class economically at best, in a small town that sat in the shadow of one of the palaces of a very wicked king. The very first people to whom God revealed the message of the baby's birth were to a group of young shepherds who were taking care of their flock of sheep nearby. A portion of our heritage here in Trinidad is built around the act of raising sheep. Portions of our own countryside may be very similar to what the shepherds of ancient Israel encountered. In the days when Christ was born, the responsibility of being a shepherd was not looked at as an honor. It was a dirty and difficult task. Often as older brothers would see their younger brothers come of age, they would pass this responsibility down to the youngest one who was able to fulfill this duty. For this group of shepherds to see the dark night sky split wide open with the voices of the host of angels singing the praises of our Lord would have been an honor they would have never expected to have been bestowed upon them. God's love was extended to all. It was announced by all of heaven. It was revealed to the kings and the wise men. But to the very poor and those without, the offer of front row seats was extended.

As I sit in this waiting room, I better understand how there can be the darkness and pains of events that so overshadow the joys of this season. I better understand how they can rob us of the joy and anticipation of what God desired to share with us. However, I also better understand the depths of His love as I come to a better understanding of His Gift to us. The people of Bethlehem lived and worked day in and day out in the shadows of Herod's palace on the hilltop overlooking their town, even as the baby that became the hope for all men and women of all time was being born in their very midst.

Heavenly Father, even as we sit in the shadows of our pain and suffering, help us to not forget the depths of your great gift of love. Help us to not forget that pure joy we felt when we gazed into the freshness of the baby Jesus. As we are reminded during this Christmas season of all that You have done for us, help us to not be bashful of declaring to others, "Do not be afraid. I bring you good news of great joy that will be for all the people. Today in the town of David a Savior has been born to you; he is Christ the Lord..." (Luke 2:10–11 NIV).

Heritage

It was the first day of spring as we headed toward the four-way stop where we planned to turn west to head toward the hills of eastern Wyoming. The sky was a beautiful, perfect baby-blue color, one which we had waited for all winter, with nary a cloud to be seen. The temperatures were predicted to rise above the magical seventy-degree mark that we knew was a sign of the beginning of spring for the year. The winds lazily blew across the plains, and the rays of the sun radiated warmth and comfort to all they touched. This was the day that we had chosen to share with visiting friends some of the beauty of this area that we had grown to love over so many years.

For the next seventeen miles, we would wind to the right and to the left of the gentle hills that make up this part of western South Dakota. One hill might be dotted with a stand of deep-green evergreen trees, where sprigs of new life were beginning to stretch forth from the tips of branches that had just weathered the winter storms. The next hill though might be covered with the tall tan strands of the dead grasses from last year as they waited for the new life of the bright green that was just beginning to make its presence known nearer to the ground below. Whereas on one hill, one might see the small herds of cattle that were feeding on the grasses of the hillside, on another hill side, one might see a small herd of white tail deer feeding in the thicker grasses of the fence rows, oftentimes with a young caramel-colored white-spotted fawn playfully running through the field, though never far from the mother who knew it so well.

After only about fifteen minutes of enjoying the experience of such a drive as this, and still nearly an hour from our destination, we came to our first stop: the town of Aladdin, Wyoming. With a population of only fifteen people, there are not a lot of places to stop and see, but there is one that has become a regular stop for us whenever we go this way. There, on the north side of the road, stands a building that has weathered the storms of the upper plains for the last 120 years. It is now home to a general store, a post office, a liquor store, a souvenir shop, and a second-story consignment shop that serves many of the locals who want to sell their personal goods and wares.

As you climb up the two or three steps to the creaky front porch, you will notice signs that will bring a smile to your face about where the liar's bench is, which bodily functions you aren't allowed to do from the edge of the porch, and what the farmers are supposed to make sure they scrape from their boots before entering the store. The old wooden screen door, which is still pulled closed by means of a coiled spring, still creaks loudly as it swings shut behind you. Inside the store, your eyes are immediately drawn to a décor that hasn't changed much since the building was first built in the late 1800s. To the right, the shelves still line the eastern wall displaying so many of the goods that the local residents still need to buy even today. The chocolate candies are sold from three wooden barrels to the right of the cash register and can be bought individually or by the scoop full. Behind the counter are the hundred-year-old roll-top bins where the farmers and ranchers from two centuries ago would have purchased a scoop of flour, or a pound of coffee beans, or even sugar or cooking beans. And there, standing in the middle of the floor is perhaps the most ornate wood-burning stove one could ever imagine. A stove such as this would most likely have provided the only heat the earlier visitors to this store would have enjoyed while shopping. It also had places where boots could be dried and platforms where coffee pots could be heated throughout the day.

As I stood in this place, I couldn't help but feel a touch of sadness at the sign I had seen outside the door to the store for the first time this particular morning. It was on this sign that the announcement was made that the Aladdin General Store, its contents, and all those things that go with it would be sold at auction in just a few short weeks. Even though I knew the current owners fully understood the unique heritage of this building and its surrounding grounds, I couldn't help but wonder who the new owners would be and to what degree would they understand and appreciate the historical picture that was painted right there before my very eyes. The question I pondered as I stood there was this: "To what degree can the heritage and experiences of one who has lived the past be passed on to another who hasn't lived through the same things?"

In the Bible, the book of Joshua tells of how the leadership of the nation of Israel transitioned from where their beloved leader Moses was the one they followed to now, where Joshua was the man whom God had called to be their leader and spokesman. Joshua walked with Moses and was one of those who was closest to him. When it came to going into the Promised Land, Joshua was one of the twelve men whom Moses had chosen to go in and see what the land held for them. When it came time to go to battle, Joshua was one of Moses's most trusted leaders. However, Joshua knew that where he had put his trust in Moses, Moses had put his trust in God. It was now time for Joshua to be the one whom God would use to lead His people and the one to whom the people would come to look for leadership in their daily lives. Is it for this reason that God repeatedly spoke these words to Joshua, "As I was with Moses, so I will be with you; I will never leave you nor forsake you" (Josh. 1:5 NIV). How easy it would have been for Joshua to have taken these words out of context and used them as a means to bolster his position of prestige and rank. Instead, Joshua understood rightly that what God was saying to him was that *He*, the God of Moses, and of Abraham, and of Isaac, would be with him, Joshua, the same way in which *He* was with the others. Where some might have used God's words to establish personal prestige, Joshua knew God was only intending to bestow a promise of His continued presence. This is the same message we need to receive from those portions of scripture in places like Genesis, 1 and 2 Chronicles, Matthew, and Luke, where we read the great lists of genealogies that were written. Does God desire for us to look for prestige and pedigree when we consider the list of faithful witnesses from whom we have come? Or is God just trying to reaffirm His promise to us that even as *He* was with our parents, our grandparents, and our great-grandparents, *He* also will be with us. How many children can look back for generation after generation and realize that those who have gone before them have served a God who was faithful and true? However, the task is now for us to take as our God, the God of our predecessors. What some may see as prestige, we need to see as a promise! Someone once said that God is not in relationship with anyone as a grandchild but only as children. Which do we seek to be?

A Way through It

While living in south central Colorado, we enjoyed having a great variety of places to which we might go in order to enjoy a day or an afternoon away. However, there was one place that always ranked high on our list: Cordova Pass.

Our goal for this day was to drive up to the Cordova Pass Campground. Driving up to this pass was not a problem due to its altitude, even though it was 11,248 feet above sea level. The problem came though, for many who would use this campground as a beginning point from which they would then make the hike to the top of West Spanish Peak, which was still another 2,000 feet higher in altitude. We knew we would be content in making the drive and enjoying the beauty of God's creation from the car and from the relatively lower elevation of the campground.

As we headed out from Trinidad to make the nearly fifty-mile journey that day, we recognized we needed to be aware of two things. First of all, due to the condition and nature of the roads, we needed to allow at least four hours to make this round trip, possibly even five. Secondly, we recognized that out of the one-hundred-mile round trip, possibly as much as 75 percent of the scenery would be less than spectacular. With these things in mind, we headed up Interstate 25 to our first turn some eighteen miles away at the town of Aguilar, Colorado. Leaving the interstate and its desert scenery behind, we began our journey toward our destination.

Even though to begin with, the journey itself on county road 43.7 wasn't what we were hoping to see on top of Cordova Pass, it was a delightful blend of gently rolling, tree-covered hills, rocky crags and bluffs, and beautiful green farmlands and fields where livestock and herds of deer and elk could be seen grazing dependent upon the time of day. For the next twenty miles or more, we would weave around one curve after another, go down one hill before ascending the next, discover weather-worn and abandoned buildings on long-ago abandoned farmsteads and enjoy the ever-increasing number of stands of trees as we came ever closer to beginning our ascent to the top of Cordova Pass.

After beginning the ascent, and traveling roughly three quarters of the way up the side of West Spanish Peak, there is one sight that is most unusual to the first time traveler and which I always found to be most incredible. Upon rounding the bend in the road and looking ahead, there, across the road from the left side to the right, is a thirty-foot tall section of one of the lava walls that radiate out from the center of West Spanish Peak, much like the spokes of a bicycle wheel. Though it is as tall as a three-to four-story building, it is only approximately ten foot in width.

At one time, this lava wall would have been a most solid obstacle to any early climber or traveler seeking to traverse this part of the mountain in an effort to get to the other side. However, at some point in the distant past when this road was being developed for vehicular traffic, the decision was made to cut an archway through this wall for traffic to go through. This archway, called Apishapa Arch, might have had rough, sharp edges around the inside edges when first cut. Now though, it is lined with limestone blocks in a manner that might remind a person of the Roman aqueducts of ancient Europe. No longer would man or beast have to either go around this solid hardened lava wall or try to go over it. Now, the path going through this formidable obstacle was safe and secure.

I wonder if the apostle Paul might have seen something like this when he was writing his letter to the various early churches. In his first letter to the Corinthians, Paul wrote these words:

> No temptation has overtaken you except what is common to mankind. And God is faithful; he will not let you be tempted beyond what you can bear. But when you are tempted, he will also pro-

vide a way out so that you can endure it. (1 Cor. 10:13 NIV)

In these verses, as well as the ones that proceed it, Paul is clearly speaking of the dangers that we as believers face when we are being tempted and tried by the hand of Satan. Even though we might not like to think about being tempted, it will be a fact of life for as long as we take breath. Satan will tempt us, trying to cause us to pull away or deviate from our relationship with our God. James even goes as far as saying, "Each one is tempted when, by his own evil desire, he is dragged away and enticed" (James 1:14 NIV). Eve was tempted, and she sinned. Adam was tempted, and he sinned. Moses was tempted, and he sinned. Even David, "a man after God's own heart" (1 Sam. 13:14 NIV), was tempted; and he sinned. The bad news is we have all been tempted and we "all have sinned (Rom. 3:23 NIV).

But here is the good news: even when we are being tempted to go against and to grieve the heart of our loving God, *He* promises that *He* has ensured there will always be a way to escape the temptation. Even as with this tunnel in this very formidable lava wall on the side of this mountain, God has made a way out for us from every temptation we face.

In speaking of Jesus, Hebrews 2:18 tells us, "Because he himself suffered when he was tempted, he is able to help those who are being tempted" (NIV), Our Father, through the life of His Son Jesus Christ, understands and knows what we are going through. And He still loves us! How incredible!

From the verses in 1 Corinthians, as found above, God has promised whatever situation we may find ourselves in, He has made sure it is not more than we can handle. What love!

Then, Jesus promised us, "I will ask the Father, and he will give you another Counselor to be with you forever—the Spirit of truth…you know him, for he lives with you, and will be in you" (John 14:16–17 NIV).

God the Father promised us that even in the worse temptations we will face, they will never be so great that we cannot stand against them. There will be an escape. God the Father sent God the Son to walk with man and live the lives we do. He understands! Then God the Son asked the Father to send us a counselor and a helpmate in order that we can walk in relationship with our God. What an amazing story and demonstration of love this is! Our Father doesn't want us to fail or to stumble and fall. *He* believes in His children and has equipped us with all that we need in order that we can succeed and be victorious in our relationship with our Heavenly Father. There can be no greater picture of what it means to be loved by our Creator and our God than this!

What love!

You All Are Invited

Whenever and wherever we have traveled the highways and back roads of this country, it has been such an incredible joy and undeserved privilege to be able to witness some of the greatest miracles of creation that our God spoke into existence.

On many occasions, we have been able to see the beautiful mountains of the western United States. At times, we have been able to see the blue-gray peaks, which reach thousands of feet up into the air, covered with the pure-white blanket of the latest snowfall. There were times when we were able to witness the beauty of the changing of the leaves during the fall, when the green leaves of the summer start their transition from various shades of green to yellows to oranges and reds, before being blown and falling down to the ground below by the mountain winds. Still, there were other times when we were able to witness the spring thaw when the snows were melting away after a long winter. The animals were beginning to scurry about for a fresh supply of food to eat, and the new growth of buds were just beginning to break forth from the branches of the trees to reach toward the warmth of the approaching summer sun.

Besides our mountain journeys, we also recognize what a joy it was to be able to see the beauty of the waving grasses of the prairie lands, moving about as the waves of the sea, reacting to the gentle breezes blowing over the land. We were able to sit on beaches in Florida and experience the beauty of the brilliant red sun setting on the distant horizon, where it appeared to slowly slip further and further beneath the edge of the water, as if it was some great ship slowly taking on water finally surrendering its last breath of life. We were able to not only witness the awesome beauty of Niagara Falls, but was also able to feel the all-encompassing thunder of the falls as it shook the ground hundreds of feet and blocks away.

There is one other aspect of being able to make all these trips that we found to be such an enjoyable blessing as well. This additional reality, which we realized as we drove these many miles in search of being able to be a witness to the beauty of God's workmanship, dealt with a very basic need. Not only do you get to see the indescribable beauty during these trips, but being as we have to eat during these trips, you also get to learn of great places to eat as you go about the country.

We found an awesome place in Tishomingo, Oklahoma, that has the best fried catfish buffet I have ever experienced. In White River, South Dakota, was a little roadside drive-in restaurant that sold the sweetest and most delicious corn dogs around. In the little town of Beatty, Nevada, the owner of the local diner makes a homemade-style pizza that will melt in your mouth. In Trinidad, Colorado, is a little mom-and-pop doughnut shop that makes the best apple fritter one could ask for. Across the border, in the little town of Raton, New Mexico, is a place that serves the best brisket I have found. Stanton, Kentucky, has a local restaurant that is known for a hamburger you can gain weight from just by looking at it. And if you are in Iowa and want to experience what an Iowa pork tenderloin sandwich is all about, I can direct you to a little town in the middle of the heartland called Wellsburg.

Even as great as all these places are, there is one other place I want to personally invite you to join me at someday. In the book of Revelation, verse 19:7–9, it is written:

> "Let us rejoice and be glad and give him glory!
> For the wedding of the Lamb has come, and
> his bride has made herself ready. Fine linen,
> bright and clean, was given her to wear." (Fine
> linen stands for the righteous acts of the saints.)
> Then the angel said to me, "Write: 'Blessed are
> those who are invited to the wedding supper of

the Lamb!'" And he added, "These are the true words of God." (NIV)

As we have shared so much time together over the many pages of this book, my one desire has been to share with you more about this one whom we call our Lord and our God. Together, we have taken trips where we have witnessed unspeakable beauties. God has been able to reveal Himself in such incredible ways through the product of His handiwork. And He did this all just to show us two things.

First of all, I believe the beauty of God's handiwork is intended to be a witness to us of how incredibly awesome is the power and nature of our Heavenly Father. How can we not stand in silent awe as we try to take in all that we see around us?

Secondly, I believe God's creation is given to us to serve as an example of his great love for us. Even as we are able to witness such beauty in a sin corrupted world, can we begin to imagine what His creation will be like when we are able to see Him face-to-face?

If, as a reader, you already have a personal relationship with Jesus Christ as Lord and Savior, my prayer is that this book may have helped to encourage you or draw you closer to our Lord as you walk with Him.

If, as a reader, you don't currently have a personal relationship with Jesus Christ as your Lord and Savior, I just want to tell you how much God loves you right now, today. Do you realize that almost two thousand years before we were even born, God sent His Son to die on the cross for us? This is what was needed so we could return to the restored relationship with our Heavenly Father that He has desired to have with us from before time began and desires to have with us for all eternity. May I have the privilege of sharing with you how you can come to receive this freely given gift from our God above?

First of all, I am not going to say "you" are a sinner. I am going to say "we" are all sinners. In Romans 3:23 we read, "For all have sinned and fall short of the glory of God" (NIV). We all have sinned or grieved God's heart by failing to do what we know is right and pleasing before Him.

Secondly, the apostle Paul tells us, "For the wages of sin is death, but the gift of God is eternal life in Christ Jesus our Lord" (Rom. 6:23 NIV). This verse tells us two things. When we sin or rebel against God's Word, the price we will pay is eternal death and separation from our heavenly Father. However, it also tells us that there is a gift or way in which we can enjoy eternal life with Him as well.

What is this gift? Romans 5:8 tells us, "But God demonstrates his own love for us in this: While we were still sinners, Christ died for us" (NIV). God provided a means for restoring our relationship with Him. It is through the shed blood of Jesus Christ when He died for us on Calvary's cross.

In Ephesians 2:8–9, we read, "For it is by grace you have been saved, through faith—and this not from yourselves, it is the gift of God—not by works, so that no one boast" (NIV). God's word tells us that this salvation we desire is a free gift, one which we can't earn or never work hard enough to deserve but is accepted only through faith in the sacrificial death and resurrection of Jesus Christ. To trust, or have faith, means we must believe.

Then in Romans 10:9, we read, "That if you confess with your mouth, 'Jesus is Lord,' and believe in your heart that God raised him from the dead, you will be saved" (NIV). God knows and teaches us that the mouth is the gateway to what exists in the heart. For this reason, He calls us to be willing to recognize that we need to be willing to share what God has done for us. But we confess only what we know God has done: He has given us new life, and He has saved us!

Nothing more is needed. Nothing less will suffice.

If I may, can I share this prayer with you? It's nothing fancy. But if this is your heart's cry today, will you join with me in expressing to our Father those cries of your heart?

Our gracious Heavenly Father, thank you for loving me so much that You desire to have a new and restored relationship with me. Father, I know I have sinned. We all have. But I also know You provided a way for me to come home, and that is through the gift your Son gave us by dying on the cross in my place. Father, I know You alone are God, and You alone can provide for my salvation. I accept this gift of salvation You have given, which I don't deserve, and I will confess with those things I say and do that You alone are God. Thank you, Father, for all You have done and desire to do. In the name of Jesus Christ, Your Son, I ask these things. Amen and Amen.

If this is the prayer of your heart, I want you to know the Bible tells us that all of heaven is rejoicing with you. Seek Him in His fullness. And if we don't meet in this lifetime, my prayer is we will meet someday at the marriage supper of the Lamb in heaven.

In His Service,
Jack. A. Droste

About the Author

Whether it has been standing on the top of a mountain in Colorado, surveying all that lays before him, or whether it is standing on a warm, sandy beach in Florida, watching the dolphins leaping and swimming playfully alongside the approaching ships in the bay, or whether it is somewhere in between these extremes, Jack Droste has always found a joy and peace in being a witness to God's great love for his children as evidenced by the beauty of his creative hand in the great outdoors.

Jack Droste is an ordained elder serving in pastoral ministry in the beautiful woodlands of upper Minnesota, with his bride, Nancy.

Together, Jack and Nancy have visited forty-five of the forty-eight lower states of America. They have stood on the cliffs of the roaring Niagara Falls and the edge of the Grand Canyon. They have walked among some of the greatest battlefields of this land. They have seen the great deserts of the southwest the blazing sands of Death Valley the calming serenity of the beaches of Florida and walked among the barren crags and spires of the Badlands of South Dakota. At every turn, Jack Droste has been able to see the majesty of our God and Creator in the handiwork of his creation.

Jack Droste has served in the ministry of the church for nearly all of the years of his life. He graduated from Crown College with a BS degree in Christian Ministry, an MA degree in Intercultural Leadership Studies, and an MA degree in Christian Studies.